Dilemma:
America in Motion

Dilemma: America in Motion

FRANKLIN V. MCQUEEN

authorHOUSE®

AuthorHouse™
1663 Liberty Drive
Bloomington, IN 47403
www.authorhouse.com
Phone: 1-800-839-8640

Published by AuthorHouse   07/12/2012

ISBN: 978-1-4685-6376-4 (sc)
ISBN: 978-1-4685-6375-7 (hc)
ISBN: 978-1-4685-6374-0 (e)

Library of Congress Control Number: 2012904862

Prologue

Those who profess to favor freedom

and yet depreciate agitation

are men who want crops without plowing up the ground.

They want rain without thunder and lightning.

They want the ocean without the awful roar of its mighty water.

The struggle maybe a moral one or it may be a physical one,

but it must be a struggle.

Power concedes nothing without a demand.

It never did, and it never will.

Fredrick Douglas

Dedicated to the Memory of:

Mrs. Tommie J. Bethea

Mrs. Bessie B. W. Nicholson

Mr. Ellis Murphy

Mrs. Carrie W. Ward

Mr. Grover McQueen Sr.

Mrs. Martha R. Boatwright

Mr. Kenji R. McQueen

Mrs. Doreen M. Davis

Mrs. Annie G. McQueen

Mr. Connell "STEP" Ward

Mrs. Anna J. Stubbs

Mrs. Betty M. Smith

Mr. Isaac "Junior" Richardson Ridges

Mr. James "Jimmy" McLeod

Ms. Jacqueline A. "Jackie" Summers

Mrs. Hortence M. Brown

Mrs. Natha L. W. Hepburn and Mr. George Bridges, Jr.

Acknowledgements

I give honor to the Creator who sent forth His spirit in man for the manifestation of His glory. To my friends, Richard Noble, Hugh Holland and James Jacobs, for the countless conversations that were a source of inspiration for this work. To Mrs. Wanda Cross, who administered tremendous patience of my countless inquires as she set this work to type. Thanks to Mrs. Kelly Dunnavant for her illustration for the cover of this book, and Ms. Monica Guilford for her graphic skills to the cover. I would like to give a special mention to Mr. Connell and Annie Ward and family, who have shared a close relationship with my family. To my friend and confidant, Dr. Edith E. Bridges, the members of the Blenheim High School Class of 1971, my goddaughters Hazel A. Bridges and Alexis S. Poe, and my long-time friends: Drayton Dease III, Perry (James) and Joseph Lucas, and Robert L. Fore. I give special thanks to Frank "Billy" David, Jr. who on one occasion, literally saved my life, and Mr. Daniel Cook who has helped in several difficult situations. To my family and all those who have supported me over the years, Asante!

Contents

Introduction 1

Chapter 1:   Prediction... 13

Chapter 2:   A Bitter Experience.................................... 19

Chapter 3:   Integration... 22

Chapter 4:   War On Poverty 27

Chapter 5:   The Importance of Education..................... 31

Chapter 6:   Manifest Destiny....................................... 36

Chapter 7:   Immigration 40

Chapter 8:   Epiphenomenon.. 43

Chapter 9:   Lie Number One "The 2000 Elections"....... 50

Chapter 10: Lie Number Two Iraq War 56

Chapter 11: Religion and the Falsification of Christianity 61

Chapter 12: Taxes, Socialism Dollars, and Common Cents 68

Chapter 13: The Peeling of the Phainian of Sarah Palin.................. 75

Chapter 14: The Militia, Tea Party, and Guns................... 79

Chapter 15: Today's Black Republicans 82

Chapter 16: How Mediocrity, Money and Stupidity Will Fail Our Republic... 84

Chapter 17: The Loss of Liberty In A Declining Empire 88

Chapter 18: Exodus 93

Conclusion 103

Appendage 117

Bibliography 121

Foreword

"DILEMMA: America In Motion"

I met Franklin McQueen in the mid 1970's when we were two starry-eyed young people who had just set out on our quest for a college education at Benedict College in Columbia, South Carolina. We were both Journalism majors. One thing that I noticed about him early on was his strong and insatiable drive to adequately put pen to paper, as he was a very serious student of poetry and prose.

Over the past 30 something years, I've read many of his works and have watched the evolution of an author. From his first publication of poems and short stories contained in *"Horizons, The Beginning And The End,"* to a second novel entitled "Once Forbidden," recounting his experiences as he traveled into manhood, he always left his readers wanting more. I knew then that his better and best works were still to come.

Therefore, after countless other poems, short stories and writings of various natures, he has come into his best. *"Dilemma: America in Motion"* gives us a significant history lesson as we travel through the maze of complex subject matter that we are forced deal with daily. We are taken back and forth from pre-civil rights to the present day and then back again. This is a necessary venture because it helps to connect the dots. This book forces us to question the "status quo," as it is designed to raise a different level of conscientiousness in its readers.

The correlations between the historically hot button items (politics, religion, civil rights, education, greed, war, immigration, poverty, capitalism, socialism, and yes, slavery too) are so well intertwined that it is difficult to take a pause from reading. Mr. McQueen has always wanted for us to not just "exist" in our America, but to "live" in it to our fullest capacity. The surest way to achieve this is through examination of it, even if we have to peel back a few layers from wounds that have not totally healed and search again for the root cause and effect. More importantly, is that those who should be, are held accountable. That in order to foster any involvement in those hot button issues previously listed, and make oneself right at the expense of the dehumanization of another, one would need to first become dehumanized. This concept is dramatically spelled out in Chapter 11, "Religion and the Falsification of Christianity."

Finally, as this work reaches the community and adds to its consciousness, I am confident that a fresh dialogue will certainly ensue. And with history continuing its evolution we look to authors such as Mr. McQueen to keep a finger on the pulse of America.

Connie Wiley-DeRamus
Tailor Made Industries,
Camden, South Carolina

Introduction

Shaky Ground

Thirteen chapters into the writing of this book, I decided to take a break amid the chaos of the sounding brass and tinkling cymbals of the political landscape, and the chatter of the virulent and obtrusive discourse, of which, in many instances, full of sound and fury, signifying nothing. To reflect for a moment to reminiscence a place and time of what I thought to be of historical significance, to the date of January 20, 2009, on the bright, but cold and brisk day in Washington, D.C., perched on the Capital steps, wherein the first African American, Barack Hussein Obama, took the oath of office to defend the auspicies of the United States of America.

From my viewpoint and analysis of that day, and continuing into the evening, I was enchanted by the festive pleasantry of the various inaugural events. In particular, the escapisms of the President and First Lady, Michelle, as they ventured from one function after the other, while performing their customary dance of the evening. In my way of thinking, it was akin to the Cinderella story. Naively, I became caught up and enameled in that world of make believe and pretension that

America had changed and healed of its dubious past of race relations. I believed in that moment of wishful thinking, that America, my home, as President Obama had advocated vehemently and eloquently during his campaign, and in his inaugural address, that there were no red states or blue states, that we are in all states, Americans. He opined that from North, South, East, and West, and irrespective of ethnicity, color, or creed, there is only one America. As he extended an olive branch of peace and cooperation to any and all who were inclined and wanted to manifest that gesture. But lo and behold, on January 13, 2009, in Chevy Chase, Maryland, at approximately 6:30 pm, at the home of Columnist, George Will, he, along with others such as, David Brooks, William "Bill" Crystal, and Charles Krauthammer, the President made an overture of peace and cooperation, and extended a hand of mutual respect, which in turn summarily resulted in, for all intense purposes, a slap in the face.

Then on January 16, 2009, came the answer from the lips of the false prophet, seeking whom he could devour, Rush Limbaugh, "I hope he fails." From that point on, the stuff hit the fan. With the mantra from every antagonist of the Republican contingency activated to stop this boy from being successful. Though he may hold the eminences of position as President, but white supremacist thoughts will remain supreme at all cost. He must adhere to our dictates.

Following was an onslaught of innuendos, disinformation, caricature, outright lies and disrespect that began to be hurled unmercifully to diminish the man, and the position he holds that was once held in high esteem, until Black began to distract from the norm.

Thus, they instituted the notion of "Just Say No!" even, if the country went down in financial and moral flames. Who could have known that deep within the current from the wave of the voracity of pride, jealousy and outrage that a black man could be bestowed such eminence. That deep within this conundrum of despair, emanated vapors that heralded insults, vitriol, disbelief and outright lunacy, from the boiling pot of tea that was emerging from certain sectors of the American psyche to the point of anarchy to reclaim their country. During the ensuing months with each stroke of the pen, and with each act of legislation consigned by President Obama, that will in the long run, enhance the lives of all Americans which has mostly gone unnoticed or ignored by the mainstream and made-up media, whose mantra has become a symbol to accentuate the negative to satisfy the appetite of those seeking celebrity and sensationalism of "Yellow Journalism."

Never mind the fact that at the infancy of President Obama's administration, according to accounts of those in the latter days of the previous administration of President George W. Bush, and the overseers of the financial apparatus were screaming that the sky was falling, to include some of those in the House of Representatives, Congress, and the Senate, who had decried the looming disaster of the financial apocalypse of our, and the world's, economies. From all accounts strewed in mathematical fact, or so we thought, a month prior to the ascending of President Obama, the economy was hemorrhaging about eight thousand jobs per month. Hence, with the commencement of the Obama administration, all financial instruments and barometers have indicated a steady increase in job productivity. But, because of certain personalities who sit on their perches engrossed in their egos and ethos, pontificating on an hourly and daily basis, seem to be incapable or impotent of disseminating fact from fiction.

Prior to the election of President Obama, there were those who were casting uncanny, disparaging and dispersing remarks related to candidate Obama, as the "Chosen One." In an attempt to de-legitimize him, first as a person, and a man who was incapable and unfit for the task of restoring financial and moral stability to the office that we hold less with luster than the previous administration, who had found itself wanting in the feat of incompetence, to navigate the financial and moral compass of the economy and the ensuing expense of two wars of more than two billion dollars a day. Not, withstanding that there was another war that had been deemed legitimate, that was also accruing substantially from the Coffers. But if we were to adhere to the cries of those across the financial, social, political, and spiritual aspects of our society, irrespective of rich, poor, Democratic, Republican, progressive, conservative, racial, ethnic, status, class, or any way you would like to differentiate, everyone stood with outstretched hands, asking and demanding what are you going to do for me? Where is mine—my piece of the pie? I want it now! It's all about what is important to me. To hell with anyone else, solve all of my problems. Stretch forth your hands omnipotent one, and let it be done. But to the dismay of the return of the one who had died on the cross over two thousand years ago, he reappeared in the wrong hue, and was instantly despised and rejected.

There were those who simmered in the boiling pot of tea, who disguised their-disregard, disrespect and de-legitimizing of the President and the office he held, as a red-herring to their oppositions to the Health Care Bill, as they ranted and raved from one medium to the other, and any other conduit to express their displeasure over the fact that they had lost their country. An entitlement that only belonged to their white contingency with a little pepper and ginger added to the disguise their true intentions of the red-herring and obliqueness of their melodrama. There are those who are gathering their guns and running through the woods parading as soldiers, readying themselves for the coming war against their government, who's on the verge of invalidating their constitutional rights and privileges. But they should take a closer look at two important events that have occurred over the last decade; the selection of President George W. Bush, and the co-opting of the precedent of financial corporations to infuse unlimited funds into the political process that was openly addressed by President Obama in his State of the Union Address on January 30, 2010, when Justice Samuel Alito recoiled at the notion that the President would have the audacity to publicly address this miscarriage of justice. Now, we are just one Zealot away from America becoming a dictatorship under auspice of the United States Supreme Court of which became evident in the latest elections. Thereby, tyranny has no favorites. And in my opinion, any justices who took a favorable part in either of these decisions, should be immediately impeached.

These are the low information voters who historically have supported and protected the same entities that brought the Civil War, the Great Depression, S & L, Enron and the financial fiasco of 2008. And on each occasion, has brought the prospect of diminishing returns, with each succession, we have had a different category of citizens who have fallen victim to the charades that have been perpetrated against them with the delusion of greater prosperity, such as the Yuppies of the eighties, Soccer Moms, Angry White Men, Wal-Mart moms, Dixie-crates of the south, and now the Grisly Moms, and the disillusioned Independents. All of whom, sought and now seek instant gratification of their selected needs.

We have the outcry of those same voices, who are vilifying President Obama because of China's predominance as an emerging power, and the declining status of the almighty dollar. Notwithstanding the fact that in 1972, when President Nixon opened communication with China, that a foundation was laid to invest in what would become a lucrative market-place for the American capitalist over the next forty plus years. Never mind the fact that at that time China was literally thought of as a third world nation. But, with the help of corporate America to concede, need and greed to invest in China's employment via cheap labor, China's willingness and farsightedness to invest in the education of its people, and a nationalized economy and the alertness to invest in its infrastructure and advanced technology to meet the urgency of the future. Hence, China has almost eclipsed the American economy, second in the world, and to whom we're indebted too.

Lately, I have heard several pundits, analysis, pontificators, and even so-called journalists rant about how and why people voted against the Democrats in the latest election. Those they assert, who reside in the rust belt in the geographical areas of the states of Pennsylvania, Ohio, Indiana, Wisconsin, etc. To include the southern red stated America, who feel that President Obama and the Democratic control congress haven't done enough to address their financial woes in relation to job creation, but what they fail to understand is that most of these jobs that have been lost, are never coming back. Just as corporate America planned and initiated and profited from, starting forty years ago to invest in the emerging markets in Asia, India, and China, their leaders had the foresight, vision, care and concerns to educate and reeducate their populace for the future. While the American people, across the board became expendable in the game of chicken to determine who would be the best player. With the aftermath of the financial disaster of 2008, it was realized that the player played the player.

In relation to all of the instruments that were used, such as derivatives, fault, swaths, or any other acts of thievery that you can codify to defraud the American people with the illusion and delusion of profiteering. It was like stacking money on the edge of mountains, and tying it with a piece of thread that broke, and the money fell off the cliff, down into the cesspool of a basin called nothing. Its unadulterated American greed on every level, someone wanted something for nothing. From the citizen who was duped and accosted into investing in one of the ridiculous zero percent down payment loans with a variable rate of interest attached to it after leaving the confines of the previous neighborhood, to invest in one of those homes on the other side of town that was constructed with three times the lumber of the previous occupancy, where in many cases, served no purpose. Or those who decided to invest in one property after the other in hopes of higher profit margin in the game that they thought would last forever. Or the so-called intelligible prognostic who became beguiled with the prospect of becoming a major player, who did not adhere to the adage or cliché that nothing from nothing, leaves nothing.

It reminds me of an occasion several years ago, when several of my neighborhood friends and I stood around a black wash pot, awaiting the frying fish that had become a custom, that was being attended by an old man who sat quietly, smoking his pipe, seated in a blemished rocking chair and poking at the fire, as he listened unnoticeably to us debating current issues on policies, social environs and relationships. When asked of his opinion of the on-goings, he responded by saying, "What you fellas are talking about ain't worth a fart in a whirlwind," said Mr. James Arthur Fennell as he continued to mind his own business.

During the course of the last year in our political discourse as it relates to the state of the economy, the mantra has been a resounding Job! Job! Jobs! and the current rate of unemployment at nearly 10%. It was an integral statistic, as it was advertised, that would determine the effectual result of President Obama's administration and the success or failure of the Democratic Congress. But, forgotten in the equation, was the fact that from the end of 2007-January 2009, there were 4.5 million

8

jobs lost, which occurred before President Obama took office. As late as December 4, 2010, it was reported on C-SPAN by the Department of Labor statistics that the economy had seen eleven consecutive months of job growth. When all totaled, since the Obama administration, the economy has subsequently improved. But you wouldn't know that if you listen to the reports that were being conveyed by those considered professional journalists.

But, not included in the equation of monthly job reports, are the number of immigrant workers, whom are being exploited of their labor, by those whom openly hail their profits, or the temporary workers who in many instances, are paid minimum wages or less, after the middle man, called Employment Agencies, get their cut. At the same time this doesn't allow for job stability, insurance or benefits. But, it's always notable how it's continually acclaimed that their profits continue to swell. Then there is the audacity to seek further tax cuts. On top of that, unpatriotically some of their profits are hidden in shelters called off shore accounts that there should be a law against it. Yet, there's still 2 billion dollars sitting on the side that need to be invested in the future.

It's amazing and dismaying that the American people can't or refuses to encapsulate the fact that American greed is the Achilles Heel, or the albatross problem preventing provisions for all of the American people. In several instances such as, S & L of the eighties, Enron and the financial fiasco of 2008, the American people have cashed in on the American dream by investing in their 401K's, various pension plans, etc. Then along came another Ponzi scheme to distract Americans from their future, hopes, dreams, and aspirations for the next generation through the process of diminishing returns and the apparatus called Wall Street.

Now, we find ourselves at a point in time as Americans, as members of the human family, at a cross road or impasse. With the latest results of the election returns of November 2, 2010, the prospect of President Obama having a second term seems to be dismal. Even though history will eventually record that he has been one of, if not the most successful, Presidents in the history of this nation. His demise, if it happens will be primarily as it has been advocated by the media, that President Obama has not put forth a vigilant argument for his policies that I consider to be another red-herring. It is not that he has not come to us time after time, to tell us that America has lost its footing. Prior to and after he was inaugurated, he has constantly told us that we as a people should and must invest in the new economy, such as renewable energy, rails, infrastructure, electrical grids, and most importantly, the education of our children, and the re-education of those lost in the failure of our Nation's leaders to prepare them for the advancement of technological change.

It's not that President Obama has not put forth and defended his policies the problem has been the acceptance that as of 2008, America had almost defaulted financially. As a result, the American people were running around, holding their heads and proclaiming that the sky was falling, terrified that Armageddon had finally arrived. If the truth could be told, President Obama has brought about a calm effect on the chaos that has lately beleaguered America. Case in point, the recent compromise he made with the Republicans on the issue of tax cuts, is a prime example. Wherein, many in his party, especially those on the left wing, have decried him to be a turn-coat and traitor to their cause. It reminds me of the Health Care debate, and the effort to get the "Public Option" in the final legislation. But, what they failed to realize or acknowledge is that five Democrats voted on the finance committee to reject the effort, thus, it was dead on arrival. History will prove that it was a wrong choice. Yet and still, the debate went on a month afterwards, wasting precious time on other issues of importance. Also, what they did not realize was the White backlash that was reminiscent of the fight for the Two Areas and a Mule Legislation immediately after the Civil War, the Civil Rights Bill of 1875, The New Deal Legislation of the mid-thirties and the 1965 Civil Rights Bill that have been a corner-stone of opposition of major legislation that have eventually enhanced the lives of many Americans.

In a state that was supposed to be as liberal as Massachusetts, elected Senator Scott Brown further diminished the chances that the Health Care Bill would be fulfilled. In collaboration with the moderates of both parties, such as the blue and red dogs, this has been a thorn in President Obama's side, obstructing his ability to move this nation forward. But, they were practically erased from office in the latest election, particularly in the South, giving way to the newly anointed Tea Party, and the self-absorbed Independents.

Moving forward, if the mentality of the Christianity of Rush Limbaugh and Sarah Palin, and the replicas and emulators (Tea Party) that is devoid of intelligence, reason, logic, wisdom and understanding is allowed to prevail, then America will rest on shaky ground of quick sand. And in that instance, may God truly bless America.

Maybe next time around, those millions of Americans who found themselves missing in action, who expect to eat from the same table of the entrée from food stamps, welfare, childcare, Head Start, Pell and Tuition Grants, Small Business, other government loans and subsidies, Social Security, Health Care, employment, and the many other social advantages that act as a conduit for private investment, may consider what God has granted you with your inception, the freedom of choice. That is also entitled to you in the constitution which offers something as simple as your right and privilege to vote. As it has been referred many times before, "You will either stand for something, or fall for anything."

CHAPTER 1

Prediction

The power of the truth is sometimes measured a moment in time until it decides to reveal itself. There are times when one suspects the truth of what is being sought after to substantiate those circumstances, feelings, emotions anxieties and beliefs about a particular event, idea or suspicion concerning proof of what it is that he or she is investing within the scope of their present condition and state of mind or circumstances.

We may ponder day upon day to seek the discovery of fact that will cause one to initiate upon a point of reference; then set in motion a force of action to resolve whatever has been consuming his or her pre-disposition.

Ultimately we want to know for certain that whatever it is or was has finally come to fruition. Now, we can say with resoluteness, *yes, that is it!* There it is—I can see it. It's before me. All that I thought or believed to be true is true. How am I going to handle it? What am I going to do with the discovery of the knowledge of truth at this certain time?

This brings me to a point of reference in the latter part of September 1997 at Warren House Apartments #25, building number 555 that is located in Huntsville, Alabama off of Sparkman Drive. I was engaged in a conversation with a dear friend of mine, Myra Cunningham and a recent acquaintance, Richard Noble, as we watched a segment of CNN News with Wolf Blitzer. I had met Myra several months past at the Von Braun Center in downtown Huntsville, a couple of weeks to this night. She introduced me to her friend Richard, the topic of conversation related to the up-coming mid-term congressional elections of that year.

Due to us being unfamiliar with each other, Richard cautiously asked me of my opinion of politics and in particular he asked me of African Americans involvement in political processes and if African-Americans should vote at all. I therefore with intentional antagonism, suggested that they shouldn't. That is if they would, they should vote for the *Republican Party*. At this point, I could see the perplexity in his facial features and the gleam glistening in his brown eyes as he stood stoically before me. He was dressed in a pair of blue jeans, white T-shirt (with inspirational print on the front and back), black and white sneakers, a waist length leather jacket and a cap to match it. The dark skinned individual of medium size and height suddenly grizzled in a way with a clinched right fist that caused me to take precaution as I laughed out loud. This only intensified his apparent disapproval of my comment and suggestions.

I then thought that it was prudent to inject my explanation at that time, so I began to explain that I had arrived in Huntsville almost a year and a half earlier. I had moved from Bennettsville, South Carolina in June of 1996. Furthermore, I attempted to express to him reasons why I enunciated my positions relating to the issue at hand. Myra stood a distance away with an apparent ear to the ongoing conversations. She stood with her 6 foot frame, her hair rolled and twisted into a ball that was befitting her cocoa skin. She had an obvious smile. She wore a pair of well fitted blue jeans, a blue sweat shirt and a pair of white fluffy house shoes.

Richard says to me disdainfully, "Why you think that?" My response was, "It's what I see, I've been watching for some time now." Then I proceeded to recount a hot day in July of 1993, after I left the field from cleaning the grass away from my okra garden. I had stopped by my good friend, Levernice David's home. I entered the modest home and passed through the living room into the kitchen to find the 6 ft. 2 in., 300 pound individual relaxed in one of his wooden chairs in the kitchen. "Hey Mac, come in here and listen to this idiot." He said with that familiar grin on his rounded brown face. "What's that?" I asked while taking a seat in one of the wooden chairs too. "This fool, I been listening to for several days that I picked up on one of those country stations. I can't listen to this guy, listen to him for a few minutes and then tell me what you think." Mr. David said with a chuckle.

For several minutes, I listened as this individual ranted and raved about the ills he saw that pervaded the Black Community. Some of what he expounded upon was true, related fatherless households, high unemployment and the lack of entrepreneur advancement etc. But the more I listened to him the more incensed I became at the condescending and disingenuous way his portrayals were presented. By this time, Mr.

David was boiling with laughter. "What's wrong Mac?" he asked with amusement.

"Who is this guy?" I asked with outrage concerning what I had been listening too. "It's some fool called Rush Limbaugh." "Rush who?" I asked irrelatively. "Rush Limbaugh," Mr. David said as he turned off of the radio. I further relayed to Richard of how Mr. David and I continued to listen daily as Rush relentlessly ranted his diatribes about what he thought was wrong with America. I continued by telling Richard that Lee and I began to witness a trend that would bring about the change of the guard of the political process and the direction it would be leaning in the coming years. I told him that we had noticed a trend occurring across America toward the Republican Party. In particular, the southern states and the states that had sympathetic leanings toward the confederacy during the Civil War. We had observed that there was a steady flow of certain politicians who had won election to office on the Democratic Party ticket, to suddenly switch to the Republican Party, to include my Governor of my state of South Carolina, David Beasley and several others in the House and Senate delegation, and many other disciples within the Black community.

In my way of thinking, at the time too many of the American people had fallen asleep at the switch. In particular, the black community, because by this time, the political pendulum had swung and there was no way of reversing its course. By this time the airways had become filled with a vitriolic rhetoric that permeated the political landscape and cast, by and large the black community as the pariah that would bring about the demise of America. The White Supremacist Mantra in the disguise of the Religious Right Wing-Ultra Conservative and the Neo-Con Zealots had convinced the majority of the American populous that the American political psychic had gone too far left and the crusade to restore true red blooded American (WHITE) values would have to be re-instated at all cost.

It was a time when there came the emergence and establishment of the militias across America. It was the emergence of the Rev. Jerry Farwell and the Moral Majority and the countless other narrow-minded radio personalities, specifically Bill O'Reilly, Sean Hannity and the like with the 'dead' thoughts emulation of the chosen one, Rush Limbaugh, spouting the virtues of good and grateful Americans (white) who valued the virtues of the Founding Fathers, the Constitution and the Bill of Rights. I stipulated to Richard that because of what I was seeing, that it would be prudent at that time if the entire Republican establishment is afforded the opportunity to govern the entire halls of government, the Executive, Legislative and Judicial branches; in order to usher in the hypocritical thoughts that would eventually pervade the political process and bring back the glory days when white domination was the 'good old days' gone by.

In particular, the southern states (Confederacy) would flourish once more. I further stated this course of action would eventually bring about the demise of the Republican Party that I fictitiously described in a conversation on pages 134 and 135 of my book "Once Forbidden" published by Authorhouse in "2005." From that night on, Richard and I would constantly engage in conversations about the importance of participation in the political process.

CHAPTER 2

A Bitter Experience

It was on that infamous and momentous day, November 22, 1963 at 1:00 p.m. that the news of the assassination of President John F. Kennedy spread throughout each classroom at school. There were whispers among teachers outside the classroom doors, where they were gathered in the hallways; and for the next two hours before school was dismissed, there was an eerie quietness that permeated the campus and study was put aside as murmurs penetrated the autumn air.

Upon reaching home that evening, my siblings and I found my grandma Hattie and mother Elizabeth focused on the T.V. set. A beige color RCA with spiral legs, as Walter Cronkite kept repeating over and over again with choked resonance, that the President had been shot dead in Dallas, Texas. Suddenly, my mother and grandmother broke into tears.

For the next several days, the death of the President consumed the topic of conversation, until the day of the funeral, where we watched intently the funeral proceedings in the quietness of Grandma Hattie's bedroom.

For the rest of the year, and the coming years, we as a family, watched in horror on the T.V. screen, the daily coverage of the Civil Rights Movement activity that was occurring across the nation.

We witnessed the announcement of the assassination of Meager Evers, Malcolm X, the countless civil demonstrations that were sometimes marred in blood in many parts of the nation; and the brutal tactics that were used for control.

In the mist of the chaos, there was the emergence of a figure that brought hope to millions of African-Americans, though everyone did not approve of his non-violent approach, that was perceived to be opposite of the Black Panther Party, that many had also adopted too.

But then on April 4, 1968, during the broadcast of the CBS nightly news, anchored by the late and legendary Walter Cronkite, there was continuous interruption of the regular casting to announcement, that Martin Luther King Jr., had just been shot dead! Again, my mother and grandmother broke down with fevering tears, and removed themselves from the larger room with high ceilings, that occupied, the two large iron beds, two rocking chairs, and a 'pot belly' heater.

While, we the children, tried desperately to ascertain the real significance of what was occurring at the time.

Days afterwards, there were the nightly news reports of portions of cities in flames, deaths occurring in the streets, looting, voices speaking out with outrage, and voices calling for calm.

A day after the assassination, a group of youth, including myself, had gathered and had also decided to venture to the small town of Blenheim,

South Carolina, which was about a quarter of a mile away from Wright School, in an attempt to burn it to the ground.

At that time, I was only thirteen years old, and had not taken into consideration, the consequences of what could have become of our intended actions. But, by the time we had gotten several yards off the campus, a blue Pontiac suddenly appeared in front of us, and blocked the narrow road. Surprised, Mr. Wade "Hamp" Prince, our principal, leaped from the driver's seat, and pleaded with us for several minutes to discontinue the effort. Finally, by the grace of God, he was able to dissuade us, we returned to the school, and abandoned our fatalistic plan.

CHAPTER 3

Integration

On May 17, 1954, Thurgood Marshall, along with attorneys, E. C. Hayes and James Nabrit Jr., successfully argued the infamous Brown vs. Board of Education Case, Chief Justice Earl Warren delivered the unanimous ruling: "We conclude that in the Field of Public Education, the doctrine of separate but equal has no place. Separate educational facilities are inherently unequal."

As a youth of fifteen years of age, I had no idea that something of that nature had occurred, or its unforeseen consequence. In the small rural town of Blenheim, South Carolina, and the surrounding areas, the motif of "integration" became the talk of the town, especially in the black community. Its relevance was resonating in discussions within our homes, schools, churches, on the streets, and in the fields.

As we, the youth began to hear of the term repeatedly uttered, and the more our parents, teachers, politicians, church, and community leaders, attempted to explain integration's complexity and implications, the more confused we became about attending school with white people. Assertions were made that white kids were smarter than we were, and on an academic level, we would not be able to compete with them. I would venture to say that out of the discussions, that probably seventy percent, if not more of the black communities were apprehensive about the thought or idea of integrating, and they voiced their opinions openly. But when the *dust had settled* on a warm, sunny morning in mid-August 1969, Freddie David, a student bus driver, pulled the big, yellow and black vehicle up to our doorsteps in Gun Island, while he waited for me my siblings and I to board it. As a matter of fact, we took extra precaution not to sit on a seat that was occupied with one of our white colleagues, to include members of the McDowell Family, of whom we had worked, played, and talked with while working the fields of the farm during the hot summer months, and who were also our closest neighbors.

The atmosphere was timid and extremely quiet. There was a death-like silence. The mere idea of white and black students co-existing in an educational environment had been tested two years earlier, when a delegation of black youth were selected to participate in a historical experiment, among them were Doretha, Henry and Arnette Williams. The following year of 1969, several other students followed suit to include Tommy L. Fennell, Jeffrey Fennell, Debra and Michael Pringle, Alexander Alford. Also, there were siblings Freddie, Sarah, Herod, and Julia David and their cousins Frank "Billy," Marian and Robin David, as well as Wilma and Ella Sue Ward and Willy Baker.

But on this morning, there was a strangeness and an eerie feeling of ambivalence as the bus continued up and down the dirt road and narrow highways, until we reached Highway 38, as we made the right turn in front of Lee Carabo's Store, to travel the next several miles to Blenheim, where we stopped at Blenheim Primary School to unload that age group. Next, we made the circle around a deep curve that led to the sprawling brick building that was once Wright Elementary and High School but now was Blenheim Primary School, to unload the attendees.

Finally, the bus accelerated forward until we were back at Highway 38 and made a right turn toward our destination of Blenheim High School, that was formerly Lower Marlboro High School.

Then as we exited the school bus, we were informed to go directly to our homeroom classrooms. Across the campus, staff members were stationed at various intervals directing and ushering us into the building; and with a sense of urgency, our eyes met to conveyed an aura of oblivion that were on our faces. The look of reservation and apprehension was notable as we scrambled up and down the hallways en route to the classes that we had been assigned. Our assigned teachers stood guard at the classroom doors as other staff members monitored the hallways.

It was the beginning of a change, an odyssey that many, after years of the status quo, could have phantom. A couple of hours later that momentous morning, we were led to and were assembled into the gymnasium to be given a pep talk, by Dr. J.S. Hearne, Principal and Assistant Principle Wade H. Prince. The rules and regulations of school decorum were espoused and our obligation to obey them.

After the formalities had been rendered, with a sense of graciousness, each former school members were afforded the opportunity to render in song, their former Alma Maters. Unfortunately, the Black students made rude outbursts after our White colleagues had sang theirs.

But rules or not, one thing had been etched in stone in the minds and souls of the majority of the black students that I had conversations with, was the proclamation that "No white man or woman is going to beat on me (them)."

During that first year, there were disagreements, arguments, a few fights, on occasion across the campus. But ultimately, the year was considered successful, and integration has become an acceptable norm among many citizens of this great Nation. With pockets of descendants who will never accept the notion of race co-existence.

Soon, we learned to play on, and cheer for the same teams, with enthusiastic applause. Gradually, genuine relations were developed, and a true sense of respect, admiration and affection for those who were once considered our adversaries. Gone were the chants of, "Black Power" and "Say it loud, I'm black and I'm proud." Etched in memory are the pageantry of our May Day events, the mandatory Senior Class recitations, the gaiety of the community parades, especially Eastside High School's Homecoming, the Spelling Bee competitions, the initiation of entry into the Future Farmers of America, the band competitions, the display of the Red, Black, and Green, and yes, the painful dismissal of many of our former teachers.

As the years have progressed, I continue to believe (as well as a large percentage of the black population) earnestly that integration was the worst thing that had affected the black community since our elusive emancipation. You ask why? Primarily, because of the financial devastation it brought to the community. The patronage of the black businesses became an afterthought. Rather than build on what we already had relative to economic empowerment, we abandoned the opportunity to further franchise that that we already had. We opted to patronize those of whom we had considered having built their wealth upon our labor.

It wasn't until one bright and sunny day on April 1, 1992, while employed as a substitute teacher at the Bennettsville Middle School off of the Cheraw Highway, I discovered the students interacting during lunch recess as they played blissfully engaging in conversation and laughter, *sincere genuine affection.*

It was then, that it dawned upon me that things had changed in many aspects, with the application of time and effort. The experience was indicative of how people if they will, as citizens of this *great* country, can open up their hearts and minds to permit the ideas, hopes and dreams that have been deferred for so long. In my observance of that encounter, I fervently acknowledged, that *if given a chance,* our children can show us to going forward. Much is to be done, but if we pay attention to future generations, maybe we will be able to learn from and support them in their efforts to come. Even though there will already be pockets of the non-committed, despite inevitable changes.

CHAPTER 4

War On Poverty

As part of Lyndon B. Johnson's Great Society initiatives was the War on Poverty, specifically, the Food Stamp Program of 1965. There was once a time, in the recent past, approximately forty-four years ago, as I reminisce, where people in the rural area of Marlboro County, South Carolina and the surrounding area, still continued to work primarily as indentured servants on the large farms. Share-cropping remained the mainstay of economic reliance for poor whites and in particular for the black community.

To offset the imbalance in liquidity, during the winter months, many families continued the traditions of hunting for squirrels, rabbits, raccoons, deer, and in some cases, opossum. They remained to fish, plant gardens, raise swine, cattle, and chickens, to can fruits and vegetables and to freeze and smoke their food. Also, to supplement their short-falls during those sometimes cold months, many families had to resort to loan advances from large land-owners, or seek support from their neighbors.

Then, one day in the year 1966, we received notification from the Marlboro County Department of Social Service that we had qualified to receive Food Stamp assistance. The following week, I believe that it was on a Thursday; Mr. Connell "Step" Ward came and picked up my parents, David and Elizabeth, to take them to town to make the transaction. When they returned in Mr. Step's car, we were able to retrieve the many big bags and boxes, and bring them into the house. Boy, there was plenty of food! You name it; there were canned goods, beans, peas, potatoes, etc.

Among the meats, we had pork chops, steak, chicken, neck bones, oxtails and sausages. The cereals included Corn Flakes, Cheerios, Rice Crispies, and Fruit Loops. There was milk, juices of various flavors, cookies, candy, and fruits.

Soon, there came the cries from certain sectors of society that blacks were now eating too good. Even among those who were direct recipients were poor Whites. There were indifference to blacks, who often worked hard to struggle to save to buy a new car, only having to hide it, especially if they were still at the mercy of their land owner, as share croppers, or where employed in the local mills. If known about, the acquisition could have had an adverse effect on their status. They could and were simply asked to move or were fired from their jobs. I can remember one day, several months later, that my parents allowed me to go into town with them to received our allocation of stamps. Mr. Step drove us to town, and parked in the Colonial store parking lot. Daddy and mother exited the car and then walked in the direction of Broad Street. Moments after they had left, out of curiosity I made my way across the street, and stood in the front of the B.C. Moore's store, while Mr. Step stood along the long stone wall about four feet high, engaged in conversation with another black man.

I watched in amazement, the long line that extended from the Social Services office, made of brick that extended about a hundred and fifty yards, down to the parking lot. In comparison, the scene was much similar to the soup lines of the late twenties and early thirties that I had observed in pictures from various sources, depicting the Great Depression. Astonishing, and to my great surprise, about half of the people standing in line, of many hues, shapes, and dress, were whites of whom were in direct opposition to the Civil Rights Act, and the many proposals out lined in President Lyndon Johnson's Great Society initiatives such as, the Food Stamp Act, the Economic Opportunity Act, Job Corps, Work-Training, etc ... It was re-assuring to see that many of the other Whites were going through the back door, either out of shame, or to conceal their hypocrisy. It was reminiscent of the Dixiecratic doctrine or syndrome, to oppose anything, and in particular, the black community, that was beneficial, uplifting and empowering. Whether it was the attempted Enactment of the Forty Acre and a Mule Legislation, public education, particularly in the south, the New Deal initiatives, Voting and Civil Rights legislation, or the Dixiecratic Syndrome, it has been and continues to be ever present in the political discourse. Whether, it was in support of The Northern Industrialist, Corporate America, Wall Street, or the Aristocracy of the South, via the New Deal, Voting Rights, Civil Rights, The Great Society,

Education Legislation after the Civil War, and now, The Health Reform Initiatives, the Dixiecratic Philosophy continues to prevail. If it's going to enhance the lives of Blacks, poor Whites, and other minorities, then hell no!

CHAPTER 5

The Importance of Education

Over the last thirty years, I have intermittingly tenured in the public school system as a substitute teacher in, the Marlboro county public school system, South Carolina, and the city of Huntsville public school system in Alabama. As a result, I have witnessed firsthand, the extraordinary advances in teaching procedures in academic and social interactions. In the Sciences, Mathematics, English, History and Vocations, certainly, we have come a long way in preparing our children for the challenges that they will be confronted with now, and in the future.

On a given day, we journey into the job market, seeking that which will make lives, financially secure. With the hope that our prior instruction has enabled us to succeed in whatever endeavor is put before us. In particular in these times of technological innovation that sometimes can defy our imagination. I sometimes, take a reflective glance in the not so distance past, wherein the pertinence of enhanced education take and remain center stage in advancing our society forward. Before all this could happen, in the spring on May 13, 1870, Senator Charles Sumner a

Republican introduced legislation that was the basis for the Civil Rights Bill of 1875. The contention of his bill would have outlawed racial discrimination juries, schools, transportation and public accommodations. But Senator Lyman Trumbull of Illinois, a Democrat, who was chairman of the powerful Judiciary committee, highly disapproved of the bill and trapped it in panel for two years. The effort had the support of Senators Robert Cain and Robert Smalls, who were black Republicans, along with the other eight black Representatives. Opponents of the bill, primarily, the Southern Democrats, feared federal funding for schools would impede State's Rights, and blocked Black members efforts to enact legislation.

A vocal supporter of the effort, Josiah Walls, felt that the federal government must educate Southern Blacks and poor Whites, because he felt the Southern States would not act. "It is useless to talk about patriotism existing in those States .... who now and always have believed that it was wrong to educate the Negro and that such offenses should be punishable by death." Walls said.

Ironically, the large majority of the Southern poor were illiterate. Senator Sumner died on March 11, 1874, and two weeks later, his bill passed 29 to 16, but the GOP defeat in the midterm election of 1874, weakened the effort. The Republican majority in the House lost in the 43rd Congress, and gave a 79 Democratic advantage. As a result, few White Republicans rose to the house floor to fight for the Civil Rights Bill of 1874, because they feared the white back-lash. But the record-breaking black representation, continued their valiant effort. "All share its benefits alike," said John Lynch, and Richard Cain sharply admonished his southern college: "Examine the laws of the south, and you will find that it was a penal offense for anyone to educate the colored people there. You robbed us for two hundred years. During all that time, we toiled for you. We have raised your cotton, your rice, and your corn and let you up braid us for being ignorant," "Let the doors of the public school house be thrown open to us alike. If you mean, to give these people equal rights of all or to protect them in the exercise of the rights and privileges to all free men and citizens of this country," declared Alonzo Ransier.

When the Civil Rights Bill came to a vote it had been tremendously weaken. "Spare us our liberties, give us peace give us a chance to live. Place no obstruction in our way: give us a chance: "Richard Cain pleaded". After the bill had been passed 62 to 99, there was no mechanism to regulate public schools. The final version greeted with mixed feelings among the Black delegation. Richard Cain, Joseph Rainey and James Rapier voted in favor, but Alonzo Ransier and Josiah Walls, out of disappointment of the exclusion of the education clause, that they decline to vote. Thus, The Civil Rights Act of 1875 was so severely weakened, that it did little to impede the creation of a system of segregation in the South, and the limited protection it did have was stripped by the Courts, "separate but equal."

At present, we find people from every profession, every walk of life, endeavoring and helping to advance our society. It is unconscionable to think, believe or imagine what it would be like in this advanced age, with all of the improvements in academia, vocation, profession, technology, etc. what would the nay-sayers at that time of debate say if they were alive today? Let's suppose that slavery still existed, and there were fifty million black people across this nation uneducated, not to mention, the amount of the uneducated poor whites, in particular in the South, where would our society be? What would we do? How would our nation be sustained? Still, we are on this perception of time, wherein, there's this talk about the disadvantages of the Public School System. If given a choice, many in this nation, would advocate primarily by abandoning the Public School System. Instead, they would favor parochial, private and religious schools. With the mainstay their financial success in numerical value "vouchers", funds that would primarily be aided by the Federal Government.

These proponents of such educational institutions would have the appropriations for the Public School System and privatize it. If this were to occur, what criteriawould measure admission? We will take the millions of students across this nation and place them in the present parochial, private and religious institutions. If so, do they have the capacity to accommodate the total spectrum of what is presently the total number to be accommodated?

Where would we get the numbers of teachers to adequately educate them? Do we start now to educate or re-educate a new crop of teachers and forget and discard teachers belonging to the present system? Who would fund the structural establishments needed and the administration thereof? Where will these institutions be placed and in what neighborhood? As a consequence, who and what individuals would be placed where and whose children would be let in or kept out. There must be criterion. If you think that as taxpayers, that if our children are educated by what we give in the lieu of taxation, then all of our children should be served.

For those who are under the belief of living a life separate from those who they feel don't live up to their expectations, should consider it an honor and privilege to have such a choice, therefore, be respectful of those who are on the opposite side of the spectrum. Continue to be involved and supportive of the Public School System despite its imperfections. In essence, be thankful that you are in a position where you can afford to make your decision?

CHAPTER 6

Manifest Destiny

I have vivid imagery reflecting upon a time when my family andI were gathered in the large room while watching an interesting episode of the television series "Wagon Train," or some other version of a cowboy or western picture.

We watched with intense excitement as the wagon trains move westward, carrying the countless number of illegal settlers to their many destinations. Whether it was the hope of finding gold, land to farm, or to establish a business, etc., they took the chance of making the journey, even though they knew in advance that they would encounter hostile, murderous and savage natives.

There were times in those portrayals that the illegal aliens were attacked by savage beast, and had to fight numerous battles for survival. Sometimes, until the cavalry arrived with guns, there were instances when the white women or girls virtue was in question. The male illegal settlers, would set out to engage vindictively to correct the violations perpetrated on them, to hurt and kill the violator(s.) There we were, cheering on the victorious illegals. As they annihilated the trouble making natives, the savage beast, barbarians, as they were depicted.

I can also remember with clarity, the study of the year in which, after being lost at sea, for several months after a violent storm, an Italian adventurer by the name of Christopher Columbus, accidentally, along with the remaining members of his crewdiscovered land.

Upon reaching its shores, they discovered that there were inhabitants already there, who after befriending them, also aided them in surviving the cold winter of 1492. Then there were other illegals set upon this land in 1619, at a place called Plymouth Rock. They too were befriended by the tribe of Pocahontas, and they also were given aide, by the inhabitants, who taught them to hunt, fish, plant and build for the coming bitter winter.

As time progressed, millions more of the illegal immigrants came to claim and subdue the land authorized by entities of governments, and heads of states that had never seen the land that they had enfranchised.

During the course of the next century, these illegal immigrants, claimed, built, cleared timber and at the same time removed the natives from what was once theirs, most times, by the force of arms. Treaties were made and treaties were broken. At the end of the day, the illegals were always justified to take from the natives their way of life, customs and traditions. But, it was not until 1830, that the official sanctioning of "Manifest Destiny," with the implementation of the Indian Removal Act, by the First President to do so, Andrew Jackson. It became the model for all, starting with the Choctaw (Mississippi) in 1831, the Seminoles

(Florida) in 1832, the Creek (Alabama) in 1834, and the Cherokee (North Carolina) in 1838.

Alexis Tocqueville, the French Philosopher witnessed the removal of the Choctaw in Memphis, Tennessee in1831. "In the whole scene, there was an air of ruin and destruction, something which betrayed a final and irrevocable adieu; one couldn't watch without feeling one's heart roaring. The Indians were tranquil, but somber and taciturn. There was one who could speak English, and whom I asked why the Choctaws were leaving their country. "To be free." he answered. I could never get any other reason out of him. We watch the expulsion of one of the most celebrated and ancient American peoples." Ultimately, the guest of "Manifest Destiny" would be embraced from sea to shining sea.

This began one of the most devastating, genocidal, and inhuman episodes in this nation's history. Today, as I travel to many places across this nation, between communities, small towns and sprawling cities, I am awed by the vastness of the land, north, south, east and west. Sometimes it's hard to imagine, despite all of this nation's advancements or visualize that this land once belonged to a people unlike the White or Black man, and other colors in between. Instead, this land was taken from them, most times by the force of arms or trickery.

"Manifest Destiny" in its truest manifestation empowered those who had conquered, the vastness of this country, to establish land barons, plantation slave owners, entrepreneurs of many dimensions, families and adventurers to lay claim to and develop livelihoods beyond their wildest imaginations, free land from sea to shining sea. The bounty of what they required has played a pivotal role in the establishing of this country, also, the free labor that was rendered for more than three hundred years. Whether it was the will of divine or selfish aggression, America has arrived this point certain. Maybe, from this moment for there can be the recognition that people of many stripes, colors and persuasions have played integral parts in its success and should share its bounty.

The official experimental application of Manifest Destiny of forcibly relocating Native Americans in the United States from their home-lands to Indians Territory (present day Oklahoma) in the Western United States, where many Native Americans suffered from exposure, diseases and starvation and outright murder, while in route to their destination and many died, including 4,000 Cherokees and thousands more from the other tribes. The sad and unfortunate passages in the Saga of American History is known as "The Trail of Tears."

CHAPTER 7

Immigration

It was a warm sunny day in December, a week before Christmas in 1971. We lived in Gum Island, South Carolina (on the McDowell Farm) where I picked my last boll of cotton. The Cotton Picker had arrived in our neck of the woods, years in our estimation, too late. It was an event that brought about the demise of small farms, to many a relief. That sector of economic output was gone forever. No one seemed to attract to the *laborious* enterprise anymore, but labor was still needed, nevertheless. So, there it was, a year later, while riding down the road on a warm spring morning, I saw one of them for the first time. I had only seen them in the movies, and I was awed by my discovery.

I hurried home to disclose to my mother, Elizabeth, of my encounter, upon which I began to give her a descriptive analysis of the individual that I had witnessed. She responded with a smile by saying, "Oh, that's a Mexican! She then continued washing the dishes.

Soon after that day, I began to account more instances of these unusual people. Years later when I started crisscrossing different states of this vast country, I watched with amazement their increasing numbers as they cultivated the fields, planted the crops and prepared them for harvest, as well as those who were picking the fruits, loading the watermelons, the potatoes, vegetables of many differentials. Later, they were cutting the grass, then roofing and now construction. As the margin of profit dramatically increased for those who employed them and wages were depressed.

For a period of forty years, a continued influx of people were allowed to occur because they were needed. Jobs that were once employed by the poor whites, blacks and other ethnic minorities were no longer appetizing. Therefore, the profound illegals filled in the gap. Now, at present, the illegal aliens are now threatening toomany who fear their presence. Many who harbor these fears are the same ones who hirethem to cut their grass, roof their houses, work their farms, pave the roads, build their houses, schools, businesses, etc. They are employed in areas that many will no longer contemplate because, the wages have been so depressed, they feel is not worth their effort.

To date, it has become an all-out effort to diminish their numbers out of fear that these people will further impact upon the economic, political, educational and societal institutions. They have become a drained on the American way of life, but make no mistake about it, you can apply whatever opposition you make like to the equation, and profit is the bottom line.

Here we are in 2012, and the issue is bound to come up at the end of this year or the beginning of 2013. The debate will intensify, when there's an attempt to wait upon legislation to either legitimate millions of illegal aliens (Hispanic people,) or send them packing. If so, who's going to pick the vegetables from the fields, the fruits from the trees, bushes and vines? Who is going to fill the jobs in the slaughter houses with chickens? Will our children be willing to cut grass, clean yards, plant flowers, roof houses, build schools and houses and businesses in numbers that will adequately supply the labor needed to cover these and other areas of employment?

They have come here and labored as Blacks and poor Whites had to at one time, but with each generation most (in some aspects) will continue to push their children to reach higher goals in education in the fields of endeavor that they have chosen. If the trend continues, Hispanics too, will encourage their children to learn more and reach higher until they are no longer responsible for performing the tasks that most of us are unwilling to do, *then WHAT?* Maybe, then we will be able to acknowledge and give respect to those who physically supply our daily bread and are willing to appropriately render to them a sufficient wage.

CHAPTER 8

Epiphenomenon

I had just driven the 750 mile stretch from Bennettsville, South Carolina to Huntsville, Alabama in a time lapse of nine hours. It was a beautiful day with a bright array of sunshine, a clear blue sky as the temperature hovered in the lower seventies. It was Sunday, November 17, 1988 several days after our family, church and community had lain to rest my dear mother

We had said our final good-byes in song, praise, smiles and tears. I was heart stricken upon my return and parked in the lot out front of Warren House Apartments where upon I removed my exhausted body from the car, leaving my personals behind.

Before entering my apartment #22, I drifted down the walkway to apartment #25, where Myra answered my knock, and to my surprise, there sat Richard on the burgundy and pink couch. After we had exchanged pleasantries, I acknowledged to them that I was going to close myself off into my castle. They in turn, expressed their condolences, I thanked them, turned and headed for the door.

When inside my apartment I quickly undressed, got in bed, and quickly fell asleep. Then, there it was happening again. I was now taking that voyage again. Upon opening the book, I began to read page after page, absorbed in the descriptive life on the plantation and the horrific atrocities that were inflicted on the slaves in order to maintain stability for the economic profiteering of the slave owner. In my astonishment, I felt so deeply, that I had drifted into an outer body experience. I was unaware of my presence until there was a knock upon the door to the study room of the small enclosure, with the night attendant, alerting me that it was lights out. This was the aftermath in which I abandoned all of my childhood teachings of humility. I therefore became loud, angry, vociferous, militant and radical in the avocation of the things that I thought and felt so deeply about and for.

At that time, I felt cheated. After twenty-three years of life, I had finally found that there was a history before Joe Louis, Lewis Armstrong, Harriet Tubman and Mary McLeod Bethune. This was an in-depth history that had been and continues to be hidden.

I returned from the Odyssey, leaped from the bed, pulled on my pants, picked up a pencil and a piece of typing paper from my desk and hurried down the walk to Myra's apartment and hastily knocked upon the door. Myra surprisingly opened the doorand I dashed past her and then I bent in front of the glass coffee table and began to draw the inscription of the map of the United States of America upon it. I then wrote the date 1619. I recounted to them my voyage from the coast of Africa at the point of no return. I endured all of the cruelty inflicted against me and the rest of the cargo, through the uncertainty of the Middle Passage. In my sub-consciousness this was actually here as the vision appeared with vivid illustration. I was feeling the pain, experiencing theexcruciating stench of death and misery that surrounded the hole of the ship. As we were stacked upon one another, as many perished day by day, while the ship sometimes violently tossed and turned.

It was the same set of sequences that I had experienced that cold night in the fall of 1975 in the month of November in one of the study rooms of the Benjamin Human and Learning Research Center (Library) on the Campus of Benedict College in Columbia, South Carolina. It was a time at age twenty-three, that I had just discovered that there were many Black writers in Literature, etc. I had avoided it until one day while venturing through the upper level of the beautiful facility that was structured of glass, I found that it was dedicated and contained information relating to Black History and Literature.

Like a child with a wonderful toy, I ventured excitedly up and down the aisles, touching, picking and peeking in to book after book until I came to the book "My Bondage and My Freedom" by Fredrick Douglas.

Next, I attempted to describe to Myraand Richard of what had just occurred, and why I was there to give to them the meaning of what I thought was its interpretation. But, when I became aware of the astonishing and confounded expressions on their faces, I immediately withdrew and returned to my apartment without further explanation.

Thereafter, day after day, and night after night, I became plagued with admonition. Day after day, I began to fill in pertinent dates relative to the building of this Nation and its symbols. Daily, I would keep Myra and Richard abreast of my progress in filling in of the map, and my distress to ascertain the meaning of what was driving me.

Then one night, one month later, I was emerged in one of my dreams, when I inadvertently, sat up in bed, and proclaimed, "The only way I will do this, is if you promise me that the Angels in Heaven will be with me." The incident paralyzed me, of which I also shared it with Myra and Richard. I was well aware of what they thought of my present state of mind, but I continued in my quest to fill in the spaces of the dilemma that was cofronting me.

Several months later on February 8, 2000, I picked up the edition of the USA Today newspaper, wherein there was a front page cover story relating to the changing demographics, particularly of the Hispanic population growth. After further analysis of urban population density, I discovered that a larger segment of the black community resided in these areas. Again, I stipulated to my concerned friends that as a result of economic, educational, political and societal deprivation, many of the former slaves and their descendents had fled north in hopes of the Promised Land, only to find that some of the same conditions relating to inequality, were not much better than the south in which they had taken exodus. Then, I surmised that if each and every individual residing in these areas were to take an active part in the political process and landscape of this Nation via Voter participation, that we as Black people could have a decisive voice and impact on the downwind of the political arena.

After my completion of the formulation of the map, out of distress and consternation, I packaged the map and a couple of articles referencing the USA Today cover story, the 2000 census, and I sent them to Minister Louis Farrakhan.

Beginning in February 2001, prior to moving to Detroit in April, I became aware of an anticipated conference, which was to take placed in Durban, South Africa, under auspices of the Untied Nations from August 31-September 8 on the topic of Racism, and the Atlantic Slave Trade.

In the meantime, while working with my brothers Wayne, David Jr., Johnny Ray and Thaddeus, at Trinity Tool and Machine Products, in Inkster, Michigan, I was fortunate enough to travel to most of the automotive conventions across the nation. I took particular interest in the seminars leading up to the trade shows. The first of which displayed a map concerning the changing demographics of this nation and of how their decisions (Corporate America) would be made in relation to the numbers. The numbers were that in the year 2040, there would not be a dominant ethnic group in this nation with the increase in the Hispanic and Black populations and other ethnic groups.

A few months later, the controversy as to whether or not to send a Untied State Representative was hashed out in the Executive and Legislative branches of our government, and the public at large. It had been discussed and was anticipated by many in the African-American community, that perhaps, Secretary of State, Colin Powell, or National Security Advisor, Condoleezza Rice's presence would be fitting to mark the occasion, but to no avail.

Upon commencement of the conference, there appeared ambiguity in some of the language used in the discourse, decorum and demeanor in opposition of criterion against Israel that likenend Zionism to racism, and language making criticism of Islam illegal. This resulted from the upheaval and the animosity of discourse that Israel, of whom the larger African-American community had paid and given homage to relating to their despicable horror of their genocide and holocaust. Whereby, the representatives of the Jewish nation, along with the United States of America and other nations walked out of the conference, wherein the subject and pertinence needed an apology and recognition of slavery as a crime against humanity and reparation for its debilitating, monumental and lasting effect on human lives.

Then approximately, three days later, on that momentous and infinite, frightful, serene and devastating morning of September 11, 2001, at 8:46 a.m. a devout enemy of the United States, Al-Qaeda led by the outlaw, Osama Ben Laden, was able to invade, elude and perpetrate all defenses of this country culminating in the destruction of the Twin Towers. It was an offense of catastrophic proportions, contributing to the diabolical loss of more than 3,500 lives of American citizens!

Wherein, thereafter, the American people rallied behind President George W. Brush, unified in its denunciation of the despicable act wherein the country as a whole joined in the resolve to bring the offenders to justice. I continue to have this vivid imagery of how the people of this country flew their flags proudly, displaying the stars, bars and colors, and spoke in unison in their condemnation of the cowardly offense, while the world offered its support.

Hence, we have witnessed an America embroiled in fractional disunity, a succession of wars that have cost in terms of loss of life, limb, blood, tears and treasure.

CHAPTER 9

Lie Number One
"The 2000 Elections"

The opposition wrap themselves in the stars and stripes of the flag of the United States of America: the red white and blue, the precious symbolic emblem of power and the belief of their relevance. They preach and teach the principles of the Preamble of the Constitution. They are the red blooded Americans who daily oppose the virtues of Democracy of this country. They are the ones who now yell and scream, "Give us back our country". Who in many corners believe with conviction that the present day President, Barack Hussein Obama is somehow illegitimate and with all of their hearts, soul, minds and hopes believe that he will fail. He will bring the America as they believe in to the brink of disaster. They are the true Patriots. They are only defenders of the value of capitalism, who sincerely believe that every American has an equal chance to access the fortunes of this country, without doubt? But unfortunately, their version of democracy was made null and void on December 12, 2001, in the United States Supreme Court decision, in the case of Bush vs.

Gore. By their own ways and means, did they unveil their hypocritical pretentions eternally, usurping the ideals, beliefs, principles, precepts and concepts of Democracy? Thereby, creating a fault line in its imperfection as long as America may exist, where Lady Justice was stripped of her robe and now wear sunshades in the dispensing of justice.

Their voices are the ones that I heard from day to day on Conservative Radio, years before the 2000 election. They were being led by the White Knight of their medium, Rush Limbaugh their chosen one, the golden boy behind the golden microphone. They were articulating the virtues of morality, patriotism, law and order, judicial and moral purity, National Defense, Monetary Superiority and Capitalism at its best, and the ability of one to raise one up by his or her bootstraps. They were the ones who believed that everyone is entitled to participate in the political process, through advocacy and the right to voice their pleasure or displeasure of political discourse, by the way of their vote, but, only for their convenience and benefit.

They are the adherence of States Rights, something that a Civil War was fought for and about, that was predicated on the belief that each State should have final determination relating to the political decision making of a particular entity or concern. That each State should have the ability to decide its State Representative, to include their electorial votes for the Presidency of the United States of America. Their voices were the ones who steadfastly advocated that every citizen of conscience should be allowed to participate in the election of their Representatives.

They were the ones who perpetuated the notion that every citizen should go to the polls and cast their ballots to demonstrate the value of liberty, right and privilege, but the more I listened to that rhetoric, the more I became aware of their farce. For instance, I was fortunate to witness a conversation while riding down one of the rural roads of Darlington County, South Carolina in the fall of 1993. The essence of which in its context, was the enfranchisement of Blacks in the Democratic Party and the extent of their loyalty to it.

Out of political correctness, I refrain from repeating in exactness of some of the language that was used in expletory, to express in vitriol their dialogue. But, some of participants felt deeply that the Democratic Party must not be allowed to govern ever again. Because as some enunciated in passionate form, that the Black man can never be allowed to gain some of the most powerful committees in the House of Representatives, such as, the Ways and Means Committee, and the Judiciary Committee. They were vehement in their objection to some of the names mentioned to be elevated to that hierarchy. They deplored the notion of Rep. John Conyers and Rep. Charles Rangel. Through their diatribes, they had determined that Blacks were becoming too powerful on the platform of policy making and some argued vigorously that this should never happen. No, not in America.

During other discussions they were fearful of the increase in Black voter Registration and they opposed any means that would make voter registration more readily available. They were aware of the many registration drives that were occurring across the nation, in particular, the Black Community. Much of the media had anticipated that voter participation would be of historical proportions.

In my continued assessment, I personally resolved the possibility that this backward way of thinking, if given the opportunity to govern outright, would possibly destroy this country. There was no logic to this madness. There had been an outdated virtue in the enunciation of what they thought this nation should be like. Its political, spiritual, judicial and societal composition should fit their mentality.

Then on election night Tuesday November 7 at 7:50:11 p.m., something occurred that would shake the foundation of this Democracy in perpetuity. Dan Rather, anchor of the CBS evening news, announced with vigor that the state of Florida had gone to Presidential Candidate Al Gore. The late Tim Russet had indicated earlier on a small black board, Florida, Florida, Florida. I can remember vividly earlier before the close of the polls, the Bush family gathered together watching and awaiting the returns. But when the Florida call was made for Gore and when the cameras were upon them once again of how they quenched and fencedat the announcement. Their expression of disapproval was adamant. This cannot be true, was demonstrated in the contempt of their dispositions. Later, they affirmed their displeasure, when they filed an official protest. From that point on, the chaos that would embroil the political and judicial limits of capacity continued for the next five weeks.

Next came the retraction of the Florida call at CBS News at 10:00 p.m. UNS at 10:16:17 p.m., 4:00 a.m. ABC News, 4:02 a.m. NBC/

MSNBC and 4:05 a.m. Fox News. All of whom had prior made the call for Al Gore at the beginning of the evening. While the drama was being played out across the nation, via the waterworks, newspapers, radio and conversations.

By the next morning, Friday November 8, 2008, lawyers, strategists, news editors, radio and television production crews were dispatched and assembled in many corners, developing strategy for the lengthy litigation that was apparent and that would emerge and put on trial the fabric of the political and judicial strength of this nation.

There were the allegations of voter irregularities, voter intimidation, outright fraud, and the protests of deniability. In addition, was the pronouncement of the different schemes employed and deplored in order to officiously deny American citizens their right to vote?

We remember the infamous butterfly ballots and the purging of voter lists, the correcting of absentee ballots by operatives of the Republican apparatus in Seminole and Polk counties, the disenfranchisement of voters by any means necessary, and the fraudulent acts of conduct by Republican operatives. All of which was a deliberate and diabolical plan to ensure favorably for the cause.

As the battle enraged, the Republican carpet-baggers, such as Rush Limbaugh, Pat Buchannan, Charles Kruthhammer, Sean Hannity, Bill O'Reilly, and the rest of the Republican spin machines tried desperately to defend the indefensible. If such blatant an offense had occurred to their Constituency, they would have probably been willing to fight another Civil War before it was allowed to happen to them.

We watched the vigorous fight that was exhibited at every level of our judicial system. At every point of contention was the relevance of the vote count. Wherein, the Republican Party stood stead-fast in their opposition to counting the votes.

In final analysis, they had developed a fool-proof plan of action. Their willingness to fight it out in the State Legislature, the House of Representatives, the United States Senate with Dick Cheney waiting to cast the deciding vote of trickery to accomplish this end. In which in any case, candidate Al Gore couldn't have won, but the Supreme Court, the last arbitrator of judicial review, abdicated their position of authority, prominence and esteem in their decision to stop the vote count on December 12, 2000.

Upon further investigation, analysis and the final vote count, Senator Al Gore was by right the legitimate heir to the Presidency of the United States of America. Despite the adherence of truth, the supporters and defenders of George W. Bush, and the defenders of the Supreme Court's decision, the main defiant in their aspiration to refute the irrefutable.

Finally, on Monday January 20, 2001, on a dark dreary and cold day, between intermittent rain showers, the reins of power of the Presidency of the United States of America was transferred from President Bill Clinton, to President George W. Bush, who took the oath of office of the Presidency and was administered by the entity that had ensured its assurance. But in the aftermath over a period of eight years, we witnessed as the illegitimacy of George W. Bush Presidency, almost brought this country to ruin.

CHAPTER 10

Lie Number
Two Iraq War

On March 20, 2003, the congress of the United States of America, made a momentous and egregious decision in passing, enacting and sanctioning President George W. Bush to use H. Con. Res. 104, where the House of Representatives overwhelmingly voted 392 to 11 to validate the legislation, and within the same day, the United States Senate voted to oust resolution s. res., by a margin of 99-0 in support of the President setting in motion the use of lethal force to over-throw, capture and kill President Saddam Hussein and his closest inner connections, a topic that I dealt with in conversation with my brother-in-law Hugh Holland on page 134 and 135 in my book "Once Forbidden."

During the lead-up to this unfortunate calculation, the main emphasis of contention, initially, and in the final analysis related to the certainty of Saddam's possession of weapons of mass destruction by the Bush administration. Even though other explanations were articulated in the chaos to strengthen and justify their ultimatum to invade Iraq. The rancor of the debate that ensued, was premised on the accusations of Vice President Dick Cheney on August 26, 2002 and August 29, 2002, that accused Iraq's leader Saddam Hussein of selecting weapons of mass destruction to dominate the Middle East (Northern Africa) and threaten the United States oil supplies.

Cheney's assertions were premised on the belief that Iraq's missile development and alleged support for terrorism were reasons enough to justifiably use lethal force to disarm Iraq. His verbose rhetoric and efforts were later supported by National Security Advisor, Condoleezza Rice's scenario of the "Mushroom Cloud." Next, there was Secretary of State, Colin Powell's testimony before the United Nations. Then the Niger connection of enriched uranium (yellow cake), the application of its use and ways of delivering it as the entire Republican apparatus stood cheering on the effort.

Little by little, the validity of those assertions began to come into question and was repudiated. Then a Central Intelligence Agent, Valerie Plame was revealed to impede and conceal the inaccuracies of the Niger report by her husband Joe Wilson. By all means, it was an act of futility that was against the law. Up to this point the media was tepid at best, in the use of their journalist skills to properly investigate the validity of the oncoming storm of war and its disastrous consequences.

It wasn't until the suspected uranium connection, did Chris Mathews of "Hard Ball" (MSNBC) began to question the validity of the accusers and in particular the Vice President, whereby the media began to take a more active role in adjudicating their vital responsibility in society.

Apprehension continued to mount among some of our Nation's leaders, who had earlier sanctioned the measure, and most of the American people. Even while questions of legality, such as, (1) if it is legal under Article 1 & 8 of the Constitution and the War Power Resolution that the Bush Administration had put forth, gave him the sole authority to enact war. (2) If its legality under International Law if seen as a preemptive use of force; and (3) the effect of the United Nations Security Council Resolution on the matter of whom President Bush, his Cabinet, the Republican regime and many of the conservative right (media) had simply determined was no longer relevant in the debate.

A March 20, 2001 report in the Wall Street Journal cited Pentagon officials saying that "intelligence reports suggested Hussein has given field level Commanders clearance to use chemical weapons and biological weapons." Secretary of Defense Donald Rumsfeld had told CBS's Face the Nation that Iraqi forces "have chemical and biological weapons and that in one case at least that the command and control arrangements have been established."

Despite the resolve of U.S. Officials international suspicions support for an early armed confrontation remained limited. President Chirac of France was a leading critic of the U.S. approach while the Iraqi issue remained before the United Nations Security Council, maintaining that he was not convinced by the evidence presented by Secretary of State, Colin Powell, on February 10 at a press conference in Paris along with President Putin of Russia, he said, "Nothing today justifies war," speaking of Weapons of Mass Destruction, "I have no evidence that those weapons exist in Iraq." France, Germany (Old Europe), Russia and China advocated a strengthened inspections regime rather than an early armed conflict.

During January and February 2003, a U.S. Military buildup in the Persian Gulf intensified and President Bush, other top U.S. and British Prime Minister Tony Blair repeatedly indicated that Iraq had little time left to offer full cooperation with the U.N. inspectors, who were not finding a smoking gun. Skeptics, including many foreign critics maintained that the administration was exaggerating the Iraq threat, and argued that the U.N. inspections process should have been extended.

After the start of the 108th Congress, some members who had voted for the resolution now felt that they were being duped and now opposed war in Iraq. Bills were proposed to repeal the authorization for use of force of military force against Iraq. The Resolution of 2002 allowed additional time for weapons inspection and the passing of a second U.N. Security Council Resolution before authorizing the use of force against Iraq.

Then in the face of a lack of success in gaining support for the resolution, President Bush flew to the Azores Islands for an urgently arranged meeting with the Prime Ministers of Britain and Spain on Sunday, March 16, 2003, which resulted in a pledge by the three leaders to establish a united, free and prosperous Iraq under a representative government wherein President Bush stated, "Tomorrow is the day that will determine whether or not Democracy can work." I can remember vividly the response of Chris Mathews in great animation as he marked in paraphrase, this guy is going to do it, this guy is going to war.

The next day the three governments announced that they were going to withdraw the proposed Security Council Resolution and President George W. Bush, the two gun long tall Texan with the ten gallon hat, went on television at 8:00 p.m. (est.) to declare that unless Sudan Hussein leaves his country within 48 hours that the result would be "military conflict," as the contingent of supporters sang "Hail to the Chief" and "Onward Christian Soldier."

Thus, on March 29, 2003 at approximately 8:00 p.m., the American people and the world watched and waited for the shock and awe of the flurry that was supposed to be witnessed in the red blaring glare, the awesome display of military might, that would result in the unnecessary loss of life, limb, blood, tears and treasure in the pursuit of Weapons of Mass Destruction that never materialized.

CHAPTER 11

Religion and the Falsification of Christianity

Beginning in (Cir. 1500 A.D.) a Catholic Priest by the name of Bartholoma de lass Casa' in his writing, in his encyclical to the Papacy said, "that these people (the Africans) were without souls and suitable for the torturous work in the Americas," the result was carte blanche exploitation justified and sanctioned by the Western Church, marking the very beginning of color prejudice. It was at this point in history that Western culture determined all evil as black and satanic, and all good as white and of God. Based upon the assumption of Padre de lass Casas, the Western Church for more than three hundred years, without any intervention, practically authorized the massive trafficking in human cargo.

The preceding passage comes from the preface of the Original African Heritage Edition (King James Version), published by James C. Winston Publishing Company 1973. Because of the deceptive overture of Priest Bartholoma, the foundation of the concepts, precepts and principles that Jesus had espoused during the tenure of his advocacy to and for human-kind was forever altered.

What makes the diabolical scheme even more sinister, was the effort put into designing and initiating into effect to erase a people's way of life, customs, and traditions from the pages of history. The same people from biblical, historical and empirical data, were the first to inhabit this world. Who by the inspiration of God, brought to human kind, mathematics, science astronomy, medicine and writing.

Throughout the Old Testament, Kamet (Egypt) played an important role in many ways in the preservation of human endeavors relating to the story of Jesus, Joseph, Jacob, and Moses. It was a diabolical attempt to stigmatize the Black race with inferiority and the suggestion of African people as being the accursed race. Ironically and according to Webster's Seventh New Collegiate Dictionary, published 1965 on page 396, a Hamite is defined as a member of a group of Chiefly Northern African people that are mostly Muslim and are highly variable in appearance but mainly Caucasoid. Then on page 132 of the same edition, Caucasian is defined as relating to the White race of mankind as classified according to physical features. The discovery of the denotation of the term *Hamite* presented me with a complex paradoxical analysis of what is truth.

Throughout my life in one situation or another, whether it was in the church, school or society at large, the inference was conveyed that because of the complexity of intellectual pursuits, we did not have optimum capacity to compete with White people (Caucasians). We were sub-human and were deserving of inhumane treatment, to be horded onto ships as human cargo to be murdered, raped, abused and used like sheep to the slaughter to be brought forcibly to an unfamiliar world and stripped of language, culture, tradition, heritage and dignity, in a deceitful effort to initiate an economy that would be the foundation in the establishment of a new Nation.

In advancing my discovery I have learned that the original Madonna was of Black orientation. Jesus himself had African-Asiatic features and is not representative of the Jesus on the cross today. Also, that three of the Popes in the initial stages of Christianity were of African descent such as Pope Victor I, Pope Miltiades, Saint Augustine and Saint Tertullian who helped to bring about Christianity to the Western World and are enshrinedin several parts of Europe. Furthermore, it was in Ethiopia that the followers or disciples of the teachings of Jesus were first called Christians thus establishing Ethiopia as the first Christian Nation and that the obelisk is replicated on every church.

Based on the premise and deceit of Priest Bartholoma emerged the infectious disease of race superiority. There was once a time and remains so today that as a result of slavery and pigmentation, wherein, I personally felt that people of African descent in the diasporas were badly affected with mental and psychological deprivation. But I have come to the realization that not only were we hood winked deceived and brutalized in the dehumanization in the concept of slavery, but that perpetrator had to first dehumanize him.

In order to foster the notion of rare superiority and to embrace some of the hideous tactics administered to maintain control of their human property it required the depreciation and imprisonment of the human soul. Both the perpetrator and those that were perpetrated against at the same time, the principles of the teaching of Jesus were preached and pronounced regularly within the Christian faith, while being able to reduce another human being to become a blank state. Countless people lived and died believing that they had neither a biblical or historical past, simply shut out from the rest of the world to travail for the next four hundred years tilling the soil and giving economic vitality to America and making way for its future greatness.

Then in 1865, with the phantomization of emancipation of the former slaves because of legislation signed into Law by President Abraham Lincoln but not after he had spoken these words during the heated debate between he and Steven A. Douglas from August to October of 1858. It was at the high point of the campaign when Douglas portrayed Lincoln as a virtual abolitionist wherein, Lincoln asserted, "There is a physical difference between the white and black races which I believe will forever forbid the two races living together. While they do remain together there must be the position of superior and inferior and I as much as any man am in favor of having the superior position signed to the White race." He believed that congress had no constitutional authority to abolish slavery in the south and in particularly South Carolina that primarily established its economic base on slavery beginning in 1771. He further stated that, "I am not, nor ever been in favor of bring about the social and political equality of the White and Black man." Thus the curse of slavery has and continues to distort the mind in relation to the soul. Lincoln, like several of the Founding fathers who devised the greatest document relating to world government and governing in the history of this world, believed in principles, precepts and concepts which are to the core. Each in his own way wrestled with the conception of slavery.

Benjamin Franklin once said, "Why increase the sons of Africa by planting them in Americans where we have so fair own opportunity, by excluding all blacks and tawnys, or increasing the lovely white and red." Thomas Jefferson in his belief espoused, "I advance it therefore as a suspicion only that the blacks whether originally a distant race or made distinct by the time or circumstance, we inferior to the whites in the endowment of both body and mind." These assertions come from the mouths of professed Christians who were considered educated men of their time. But in my opinion they are either lying, ignorant, fools or twice.

On each occasion the economic equation stood center stage. The economic advantages outweighed moral justice and principles. Lincoln, like his predecessors at one time or another, openly advocated for the institutions of slavery, wherein some were slave owners and Christian. President Lincoln out of necessity of the moment in order to save a fractured Nation made a momentous decision that cost him his life, and that is, he had taken away a way of life of economic viability and empowerment from the South.

After the war had ended these people who had languished in the official endorsement of oppression of slavery were now left to wonder in the wilderness without land, education and economic empowerment. Deprived of their Forty Acres and a Mule, most sought refuge in the *Promised Land* of the north still illiterate and ignorant of the system that was not devised to encompass them as citizens. They were made to experience some of the same racial disparities and attitudes that they had hoped to escape from their exodus from the South.

One hundred years after emancipation with the enactments of the 1965 Civil Rights Act, for the first time the Africans who were forcibly taken from their original homes and made to build this economy, north, south, east and west, finally had some measure of law that would shelter them from the random loss of life and from the murderous hands of lynchings, rapes and injustices of many stripes. We were like a people just being born. From nowhere, we had to find a way to go somewhere amidst the staunch opposition to every measure of advancement while trying desperately to shed the stench of the holocaust of slavery in this Christian Nation.

Under the percepts, concepts and principles of Christian belief is the offer of redemption and recompense. In the name of Jesus, a full admission or acknowledgement of a previous wrong. In a recent move toward this admission, the congress of this nation, both the House of Representatives and the Senate made a cowardly displace of attrition under the cover of darkness to make amends for dereliction of the past sins.

February 1, 2010 marked another episode in the acknowledgement of Black History and African-Americans contributions in the establishment and preservation of this Nation know as Black History Month. There were people, places, events, things times and places recited upon as having made a positive impact upon the history of this Nation. But some figures will be left out because they were not considered palatable influences to present day discourse, such as Demark Vesey, Marcus Garvey, Paul Robeson and many others who by their own measure tried to bring about the true measure of emancipation of mind, body and soul in the appreciation of *self*, who in many ways have been excoriated from the pages of American History because of their approach to empowering their people, in essence they were no less a patriot than Nathan Hale before being hung declared, "Give me liberty or give me death."

CHAPTER 12

Taxes, Socialism Dollars, and Common Cents

Let us imagine for a moment a fictional character who grew up in the back woods of South Carolina, who also worked as a share cropper in the mid-sixties on one of the remaining plantations, from sun-up to sun-down gathering of the crops for a measly $2.50 to $5.00 a day, either picking cotton or cropping tobacco, and only on rainy days, was he or she allowed to attend school. During the early Fall months, in hopes of attaining a proper and valued education with a high school diploma, by the feeding, fostering, nurturing, expansion and facilitating growth of his or her mental ability to prepare the establishment of the foundation of future pursuits and endeavors.

Then with the help and support of family, teachers, principals, church, community friends, associates, the state and nation, he or she after twelve tortuous years of concentrated study, is ready to make a choice to plight and charter a course of what will become the rest of his or her life. Let's suppose that the character in question, upon graduation, was able, blessed and honored with the privilege to be accepted to a prestigious university to continue his or her education.

To financially facilitate the accolade that has been bestowed upon him or her, as a consequence the individual received a Pell Grant, a Tuition Grant of some kind, work study, several foundational grants, assistance from family, church friends, and associates. As a result, the individual was able to tenure an undergraduate degree, a Master's degree, and a Ph. D degree in the specialized field of Business Administration. Afterwards, he or she further applied for and was able to receive a substantial loan (after the dotting of the I's and the crossing of the T's) from the Small Business Administration and other sources to move forward at the crossroads to succeed with the task at hand.

Upon the piloting of the project and it was off and running, customers from the community that he or she had returned to began to flock in and out of the facility daily. People, who previously supported the individual, family churches and community, were now buying the products that were offered. Then five years later he or she finds financial stability. He or she is now financially secure and is able to purchase a home, a new car, a boat, an RV, another plot of land, buy new clothes and go on extended vacations.

With the aftermath of reaching million dollar status, the individual receives their annual tax assessments relating to community, State and Nation. Whereby, he or she becomes subdued and remorseful by the bracket and the amount of taxes that's levied against him or her. The responsibility somehow appeared unfair to the individual, not, withstanding the fact that he or she had stood upon the shoulders of the many others in order to have achieved their present position or status in society.

He or she is now unmindful of the help and support of family, educators, church community, State and Nation that aided them in attaining the achievement. He or she is no longer mindful of doing unto others, as you wish done unto you, of doing unto the unfortunate among us. No longer does he or she believe in loving thy brother or sister as they love you.

The example espoused, grows deeper and broader across the spectrum of our society pertaining to the need and responsibility to pay their fair share of taxes. Sometimes, it amazes me concerning the chatter I hear daily in the media, the voices that are in opposition to paying taxes, who feel that they are adversely affected financially by government intrusion in their lives.

But, I wonder if any of them were educated in the Public School System, received financial assistance to further their education, received a loan from the Small Business Administration or some other governmental entity through subsidy to continue farming, or some other Corporate entity to defray taxes for a length of time, or to be bailed out after endangerment of failure through greed.

Maybe you are employed in one or another facet of local, state or federal government receiving a substantial salary that is only possible by the tax-payer across this Nation, no matter how low on the totem pole they are. You may receive food stamps or some other governmental assistance but, it is always about one hand washing the other. Furthermore, you want decent roads to ride on, community centers and parks. We are comfortable building other nations while at the same time our financial structure and infrastructures are failing. We pride ourselves in the building of schools, financial institutions and armies in Iraq and Afghanistan, while opposing the same domestically.

Regardless of whether you are employed in government or the private enterprise, the success you receive is dependent on the support of others. You may be an entertainer, an athlete, an entrepreneur etc., but, the financial success you received would not be possible if other people did not fill the clubs, arenas, stadiums and businesses from all levels of society to have aided in the success no matter how gifted or intelligent, you are. There may be some of you who are able to travel to some of our national parks, waterways, monuments, arenas, or stadiums etc., across this nation that are subsidized in part or in full by local, state and federal revenues (taxes). Unfortunately some of the privileges you may enjoy, may never be enjoyed by others who pay taxes, no matter how menial it may appear to you who are privileged financially who my enjoy such comfort. Because of their status on the lower end of the totem pole, the taxes that they contribute no matter how trivial it may appear to you still adds up to dollars and cents.

There are those who proclaim to be the ultimate patriots who after all of the success that they have achieved and received continue to hide and hoard their financial success in Off Shore Banks in the Cayman Islands and Switzerland and other tax shelters. At the same time our country is in financial decay, distress and collapse. *Greed and selfishness has brought our country to financial paralysis.*

Sometimes, I am appalled at the degree of stupidity that the trickery of trickle-down economics has not worked. Remember that taxcuts under President George W. Bush's administration and their contention was for a period of eight years that if the rich top two percent would receive substantial tax breaks and cuts that they would reinvigorate the market and reduce the federal deficient. Remember?

There are those who continue to blame the financial ills of this failing economy on the less fortunate among us. Those who are employed through Employment agencies who offer low wages for part-time employment, no health benefits and no labor or lack thereof, continue to bolster the profit margins of many business entities. Many radio and television personalities operate and succeed financially on disinformation and the ignorance of thepeople that they purport to champion.

Since President Barack Obama's ascendency there has been all of this talk about socialism and the devastating affect that it will bring to the diminishing of our economy, and of how the increase of raising tax revenue would have an adverse effort in the day to day operations of the free enterprise system. Nearly a month ago I was watching the History Channel about 6:30 a.m. and there was a documentary conveying the conception, inception, construction and implantation of the Manhattan Project and the Atomic Bomb, and it's devastating impact on humanity. But its possibilities could not have been realized without the taxpaying citizens of this country. Plus the fact that it would rely on borrowed money to finance such an ambiguous project.

To further accomplish this featwithin a period of a couple of years, entire cities such as Oakridge, Tennessee, and Los Alamos, New Mexico were established with still-fullness. Those entities survived and flourished at time when the rest of the economy was experiencing a depressed environment during the time of World War 2. Combined in the apparatus of the Manhattan Project, ultimately thousands of people were employed, thousands of homes were built and massive structures established to facilitate the research and development of the Atomic Bomb. Though the financial outlays were first financed by the taxpayers and borrowed money that would have to eventually be accounted for and be repaid by the tax-payers who were impervious to its clandestineness, ultimately its simulative affect for private enterprise led to the establishment of businesses of all kinds. Whether it was a store, a bank, roads being paved, or electrical lines extended, altogether people were put to work and supported by the financiers called tax-payers, in which was brought about and based on socialist theories, a collective means of accomplishing a desired goal of affect.

During and after World War 2 the Department of Defense establish a chemical monition manufacturing and storage plant, and under the instrument of Eminent domain, land was consociated from its owners, thereby establishing the facility of the Red Stone Arsenal in 1942. Prior to that period under the umbrella of the New Deal under the auspices of President Theodore Roosevelt, the Tennessee valley authority was established, whereas dams were in the built north, south, east and west to facilitatehydroelectric generation. Then and after World War 2 a local native, Senator John Sparkman and Dr. Weber Von Braun, would lead an effort to develop the rocket that would lead to putting the first man into space, and now accommodates the U.S. Army Ballistic Missile Agency, the U.S. Army Missile Command, the U.S. Army Space and Strategic Defense Command and the Marshall Space Flight Center. Without the practice of social engineering, this city of more than two hundred thousand inhabitants that covers a land area of 174 square miles would not be possible today.

As a result of these facilities, Huntsville, Alabama has been designated by the Employment Review Magazine, as one of the best places in the United States to work and live. Among 50 fortune 500 companies in the private sector who have relied on and thrive on this socialization are; Boeing, Engelhard Corporation, Daimler Chrysler, SCI System, Intergraph, Ad Tran, among others. Among these institutions and the 1,300 industrial firms and organizations they employ thousands of people, both domestic and foreign! But we must acknowledge that without the initial revenue generated by the U.S. taxpayers, none of it would have existed. It is our collective offering that has made it all possible for others to live, work and thrive in an almost collapsed economy.

The success of this Nation is incumbent on the recognition and responsibility that one hand washes the other. And until this recognition is actualized, this Nation will continue in financial paralysis that it has experienced over the last two decades, with no end in sight.

CHAPTER 13

The Peeling of the Phainian of Sarah Palin

On September 3, 2008 at the Republican National Convention, an unknown attractive and bubbly woman by the name of Sarah Palin, Governor of the state of Alaska, audaciously adorned the stage as she stepped to the podium. She electrified the crowd as they rendered enthusiastic applause, who were embellished in the vociferous and thunderous roar in the facility of the Xcel Center in Minneapolis/ Saint Paul, Minnesota to deliver a fanciful address to the cheering, engaged and illuminated audience, to listen to what they hoped, believed and prayed would be the salvation of Senator John McCain's failing candidacy.

Prior to that moment, I had heard her name mentioned several times on Fox News Network by none other than Williams (Bill) Crystal, an analyst for the network. On those occasions he would rave reverently about her credentials that he thought would qualify her to be Vice-Presidential material with the possible chance to become President. I was listening to the comedic articulations in my room across the hallway from my friend

Richard's room, where he was engrossed in the anticipation of what unfortunately turned out to be a discourse void of substantial value.

When the performance was finally over, I heard a knock on my door, Richard was inquiring of my critique of the vitriolic display. My response was to give it a couple of weeks. Sure enough after a couple of weeks and beyond of examining fact from fiction, with Charlie Gibson's interview, anchor of the ABC Evening News and the interview with Katie Kuric of the CBS Evening News, any intelligible and informed individual should have been able to see through the facade of the farce that was attempted to be perpetrated on the psychic of the American public. The empty virulent rhetoric, condescending assault of character assassination and wishful thinking that was being brought to bear with the shallow and uniformed nature of Sarah Palin's demeanor.

You would not have known it the next morning on Morning Joe's of MSNBC and Fox News because personalities such as Pat Buchannan casted her as the Great Coming. He was embroiled and enthralled with the one liner catch phrases and innuendos. As the weeks continued, many in the media were caught up in the euphoria of personality and raved about the antics Sarah Palin had employed in her performance. After discussion, analysis and evaluation, I concluded I'd heard nothing rendered of substantial value. The absence of intelligible thought about the plans, ideas and solutions for the ills that faced the Nation at the time was *profound*.

Several weeks earlier an awful decision had been made to purport Sarah Palin as Vice Presidential candidate to Senator John McCain. She had become the darling of the dinosaur of politics, Pat Buchannan, a continued aspiration of the Southern Strategy, along with a contingency of the Republican Party's elite, while in the face of reputable evidence this woman was not qualified to possibly be President to be led by the nose unaware, uninformed and unequipped about the factors concerning domestic and foreign affairs.

Before the race was over along came, Joe Wurzsbache "The Plummer." where, he and Sarah Palin became the faces representing the Republican Party. Whereby, Joe the Plummer and Sarah Palin became the Republican Party's last great hope. At the end of the day, most Americans had concluded that Sarah Palin had no chance there. But the false prophesy of Rush Limbaugh, the unintelligible aspirations of Sean Hannity, the deceitful and contemptible assertions of Bill Crystal, the hopefulness of Bill O'Rielly, the craziness of Dick Morris, the backwardness of the Southern Strategy of Pat Buchannan and the stupidity of Glenn Beck and all those who continued in the perpetuation of the invention of White Supremacy, relentlessly supported the myth of Sarah Palin to the ballot box.

As the saga continues, Sarah Palin has found her rightful place in the area of show business. Her celebrity has brought her both fortune and fame. She remains a great rally cry to captive audiences, some of whom remains steadfast and faithful that she will someday lead this Nation as President. In my humble opinion, if that day should ever occur, it will be all that is left to say about where we have reversed in time. Back to a time of reincarnation of the famine version of the personalities and philosophy of George Wallace, David Duke, and the Southern Strategy of divide and conquer. It will be interesting and eye opening as we continue to play the game of show and tell with affairs that will affect this Nation for future generations.

CHAPTER 14

The Militia, Tea Party, and Guns

In the early hours of April 17, 1995, at approximately 9:02 a.m., was the tragedy of the bombing of the Alfred P. Murrah Federal Building in Oklahoma City, Oklahoma by a disgruntled and deranged American by the name of Timothy McVeigh. As a result of the monstrous, diabolical and cowardly act, 168 Americans were confirmed dead. Nineteen of whom were children, who were at America's Kids Day Care Center within the building.

McVeigh later justified his killing of the children in the bombing; "I didn't define the rules of engagement in the conflict. The rules, if not written down are defined by the aggressor. It was brutal, no holds barred. Women and children were killed at Waco (Texas) and Ruby Ridge. You put back in [the government] exactly what they've given out." Moreover, more than 680 people were injured. The majority were abrasions, severe burns and bone fractures.

Months prior to this dastardly and horrific event, it was being reported in many media outlets, i.e.: radio, television, newspapers, etc., that there were increasing numbers of people becoming involved in militia groups across the nation. These people were engaged in preparing for what some thought, believed, and still believe is the impending war between the races that will cleanse America of all ethnic elements that is diluting the purity of the White race.

Now with the advent of President Barack Hussein Obama, such groups have emerged once again, with a vengeance. Weeks after the inauguration of America's first black President, it was reported that there was an increase in gun sales, ammunition, and numerous threats against the President's life. At the same time, there has emerged a new group of patriots (Klansmen) under the disguise of the Tea Party, who are admonishing that they want their country back. They are espousing that their way of life has been threatened. That their life, liberty, and pursuit of happiness are a bygone remnant of yesterday. They have uttered vitriolic slurs, innuendo, caricatures, hate, jealousy, disgust, distrust, despise, and the venomous acts of disrespect at the President, based on frivolous and unfounded contentions.

Once again, they are stockpiling their guns and ammunition, while being manipulated and exploited by the carpet-baggers of the gun industry and lobbyists, who are capitalizing on ignorance and stupidity. I can understand and respect an individual who purchases a gun for safety and leisure. But the audacity to assemble stockpiles of assault weapons for what purpose is beyond my way of thinking. Yet they complain about the difficult economic straits that they find themselves in. Money that can possibly put food on their tables, or defray cost in some other way, other than waiting around to use them in ways that are unbecoming, such as preparing for war against their Nation, without merit. If that be the case, then who will fire the first shot? And with what consequences?

Let's not forget the lesson of John Brown, the Civil War, the Whiskey Rebellion, and all of the destruction that they incurred in lives, limb, blood, starvation, disease, etc.? What now?

CHAPTER 15

Today's Black Republicans

In preparation for writing this book, I have examined research related to Black's involvement in the Republican Party. I can understand why, after the Civil War, Black's tried to find a way to assimilate into the fabric of American society after President Abraham Lincoln emancipated the slaves, even though he was initially opposed to it.

But, the affinity towards the Republican Party for Blacks was primarily based on that premise. Then there was that battle of and for the Civil Rights Bill that was ratified in 1875, primarily articulated by 10 Black Senatorial Representatives, who sought and fought for the establishment of public accommodations and public school improvements. During the process of that long and bitter debate, White backlash in the north and south against its passage became virulent. So was the right to approve the Forty Acres and Mule legislation. With every effort to improve the enhancement of the plight of former slaves, the White backlash ruled the day.

We can advance to the fight over and over for the New Deal Legislation, under the administration of Franklin D. Roosevelt, the 1964

82

Voting Right Act, the 1965 Civil Rights Act, always the psychic of the invention of the disease of White Supremacy remained, and remains an impediment to true progress of American prosperity for all.

Presently, we have this battle by the Tea Party movement in disguise of the constitutionalist, States Rights advocates and unfair taxation. Tip, tip White Supremacy. We are now embroiled in a battle over Health Care, with the same backlash but now they are called Independents, one in particular that I consider the reincarnation of Ralph Nader, John Avlon. Make no mistake about it, it is an affront to delegitimize the first Black President. We're in a battle that will set the course of America moving forward, or we'll relent to the pre-historic psyche of the Dixie-crats, the Southern Strategists, and now, the Tea Party members who will fight to the end to defend the corporate, capitalists, and the Southern Aristocracy who will keep them in servitude as indentured servants. Who are victims of the political propagandists as they remain, political gypsies, who have co-opted the Republican Party.

Therefore, the Black Republicans of today, who constantly defend the Tea Party Republicans and their shenanigans are no better than those Blacks who history has alleged that took an active role in the enslavement of those human beings, who were stolen from Kamet, Ethiopia, and/or Africa.

CHAPTER 16

How Mediocrity, Money and
Stupidity Will Fail Our Republic

It was January 1976, that as an aspiring student of Journalism, I took the course "Introduction to Journalism." Of which, the main emphasis or motif of the subject matter was centered on who, why, where, when, and sometimes how of developing a story. Translation, a composition based on facts.

As a point of inspiration, I reflect to my childhood, when each evening, my family and I would gather around the television set to watch the CBS Evening News, anchored by the late and distinguished Walter Cronkite. One who had attained the statue of integrity in his field endeavor, along with others, such as the late Harry Reasoner and Roger Mud, and the late Mike Wallace, the late Timothy J. Russert, and the late Edward R. "Ed" Bradley.

Those voices were and are the epitome of what a true Journalist was and should be, those who factually disseminate information to the general public without prejudice or bias with issues and concerns affecting our daily lives.

When it comes to the issue involving Watergate and the discoveries revealed by Carl Bernstein and Bob Woodward, and as excruciating the facts were to the country, President Richard M. Nixon had to resign in disgrace from the Presidency of the United States of America, based on the truth that had been brought forth.

Then there was the debate of the 2000 election, of which against all legal and historical precedent that the United States Supreme Court was allowed to choose or select the President of the United States of America. Never mind the schemes and illegalities that were implored to deprive American citizens of their entitlement to vote in this Republic that operates on the premise of Democracy. After which, the nation went silent. Not even the media, the so called arbiter between the government and the people attempted to pursue and present to the American people, the underlying facts and truths that led to the tragedy of the abominable, veil and wicked miscarriage of justice. This issue should have been kept front and center to this day with a barrage of news stories, opinions, and documentaries, in attempts to explain to the American public of how this dastardly deed created a fault-line to our perceived Democracy.

Next came the question of the Iraq war, and the looming and penetrating question as to the validity and rational that the Bush Administration was hell-bent on taking this country into an unnecessary and illegal war that violated international norms of law. The media by and large became embroiled in the hyperbolic and euphoric atmosphere of the moment and became negligent in their duty as arbiters between the people and the government to factually report the disparities in the administration's argument to go to war. Therefore, allowing the majority of the American people to fall hook, line and sinker in the marasmus of that veil, deceitful and wicked proposition. In the course of the deliberations, a CIA agent was betrayed, lies were made to the United Nations General Assembly and the American people. Allegations of erupting Mushroom Clouds, Weapons of Mass Destruction, Chemical Weapons and carriers, and let's not forget the good old delicious "Yellow Cake" extortion. All to no avail, which have led to the loss of unnecessary lives, limb, blood, and treasure.

It appears that the media at large have become a victim of Corporate Colonizalization and its influence by the power of the flue strings to effectively effectuate the lawlessness of that misadventure in American history.

Let's not forget the case of the fox guarding the hen-house scenario at Fox News, where many of the artificial news people, analysts, pundits, commentators and their stupendous and idiotic followings who cheered and facilitated this atrocity without regard for factual inquiry. It appeared in some cases that people like the Koch brothers, Rupert Murdock and Donald Ailes discovered and bought up fools like Rush Limbaugh, Sean Hannity, and the rest of the fools on conservative radio, television, and some aspects of the printed media to fool the uninformed.

Most recently, there was the case of Citizens United vs. The Federal Election Commission, whereby, the United States Supreme

Court, decided in a landmark case in a 5-4 vote that corporations can act as individuals in their ability to infuse unlimited amounts of cash in the political system via political groups that are unaccounted and unaccountable for disclosure, in an attempt to sway election(s) that best suits, and give difference to their interest. As a result of the 2010 elections, there's a mandate to fulfill an obligation to control or eliminate the hard fought for and earned rights of the conscientious workers of America of the right to collectively bargain for fair wages, benefits and entitlements as contributors to those who continue to profit unabated as a result of the Bush taxcuts, the Wall Street Bailouts, the expatriation of capital into Off Shore Accounts, Tax Loop Holes and Tax Breaks that allow them to keep the American people under sway of the tutelage of serfdom.

Lately, some have suggested and surmised that the privileges and the efforts on behalf of the Aristocrats are unethical and immoral, and furthermore is *wicked*!

CHAPTER 17

The Loss of Liberty In A Declining Empire

Over the past two years there has been a ground swell of rancor, filled with vitriolic rhetoric emanating from the vicious voices of those who feel vehemently that they have lost their country and certain liberties. That their liberties are being taken away and that their children will inherit a country far different than the one that they have been privileged to enjoy and are used too. None of which are obvious at the time. They have espoused the virtues of fewer taxes, less spending; kill the bill of health insurance for all Americans, and more guns and ammunition for the impending revolution. But, when weighed in context of its contents based in reality, it can be equated to a verse taken from one of the late James Brown's songs, "Talking Loud and Saying Nothing."

Beginning in 1972, President Richard M. Nixon, for the first time in memorable history, gendered a dialogue with China, thereby unleashing the unlimited and untapped potential for the furtherance of "Corporate Colonization." It was an opportunity for the corporate leadership to lick their chops of the colonization of strategic planning and implementation of a course of action to invest in the vastness of cheap labor. This helped in divesting them of the obligation to forewarn the American worker that the future for profitability would no longer involve them. They omitted to reveal that Asia, India and China were educating and re-educating their populous for the advancement of new technology, and the like.

Almost three decades later, President Ronald Reagan attempted to underscore this assertion when he zealously interceded to stop the Air Traffic Controllers Union in 2002, whereby an ambulance of propaganda circumventing the importance of collective bargaining emerged with vigorous contempt and continues to this present day. And all of those voices that take part in this escapade are deceitful at best.

Lost in confusion is the reality of those who fought, shed blood, sweat, tears, suffered and died for better working conditions, safe working environments, health care insurance, better wages, holiday pay, medical leave, maternity leave, and the creation of the "Middle Class," in which had a positive and direct effect on employment in the right to work states. But with the advent of lucrative markets in Asia, India, China and elsewhere in the world, it has led to a cause and effect of joblessness here in America as Corporate America's Colonization of economics are more favorable to their appetite and the bottom line of profit. Yet, they have the gall to ask for fewer taxes, and the threat of ex-patriotism while they continue to expatriate their capital in Off Shore Accounts and refuses to invest the two trillion dollars that is sitting on the sidelines as a direct result of the taxpayers of this country bailing their 'behinds' out after they had stepped in their stupor of greed.

During the recent visit of President Ha Cheng Tie, much has been said disparagingly about the debt that our country has incurred with that country and what flexibility we have in negotiating terms of expanding into and capitalizing in the Chinese economy. According to capitalism 101, at the end of the day the better hand wins. If you don't believe it, miss a mortgage payment, a car payment, or be late with a credit card bill, utility bill, etc.

After forty years of a declining economy, misguided and unwise leadership in government and corporate entities, the blame of it all seems to rest in the hands and falls at the feet of our present President Barack Hussein Obama. Many patriots of our country feel that he's un-American and who has attempted to de-legitimize him in various ways. He's depicted as one who doesn't share their values, or empathize with their pain that was created before he came along. But, the attempt to caricature him in such a way as to diminish his integrity to be acceptable has been and continues to be an unrelenting mantra.

As of today, the airways and pages of the media are filled with the discrimination of what is happening in Egypt and the desires of the Egyptian people's thirst for Democracy. But lost in the euphoria and expletive zeal is the melee of the 2000 election when George W. Bush was selected by the United States Supreme Court. But, more vexing was the underlying factors of voter intimidation, voter fraud, voter suppression, and all of the other schemes that were used to deprive American citizens of the right to vote. Such acts should have propelled every conscientious and righteous citizen to have become active and filled the streets, highways, by-ways, paths, passages, alley-ways, corridors, parking lots, etc. to deny the injustice, but the nation as a whole succumbed to the hypocrisy.

To add insult to injury, on January 21, 2010, the United States Supreme Court decided in the case of Citizens United vs. Federal Election Commission No. 08-205, that corporate entities were to be considered as persons, thereby opening a floodgate of money of known and unknown entities to buy and sell at will, the political process. Recently, there has been an attempt in the House of Representatives to disallow public campaign financing. And now we await the pending litigation of the Health Care Legislation that will once again be decided by our revered Supreme Court, the final arbiter addressing law pertaining to justice or injustice in this nation. Hopefully, they will somehow reasonably recognize and conclude that "Single Payer" is the solution to our present health care crisis.

Taken in its totality by those who are whistling in the dark, expressing their desires to have their country back and buying up guns and ammunition for what they consider the impending revolution. If the United States Supreme Court has its way with an additional zealot of political activism, then the tea they are drinking may turn out to be bittersweet as they continue the pursuit to maintain and perpetuate the mantra of White Supremacy.

Recently the citizens of Wisconsin have actualized to their regret after voting in a Republican majority, who are now attempting and will possibly prevail, in denying them of their right to collective bargaining.

They got caught up in the Wisconsin Sleepers, They closed their eyes and minds a moment too long and were awakened to reality.

As we move forward to the election of 2012, it may do us well to take a long hard look at the legitimacy of the "Electoral College" in the districts that we live in and for the purpose that it serves and of all of our elected representatives, true Democracy.

CHAPTER 18

Exodus

On January 1, 1863, President Abraham Lincoln set into motion a momentous decision with the signing of the famous document known as the "Emancipation Proclamation" after bitter debate and apprehension for setting free the slaves that had labored and languished in bondage since the recorded date in1619. With the stroke of his pen that ultimately costs him his life on April 14, 1865, when he was unfortunately assassinated by John Wilkes Booth, a confederate sympathizer.

History has indicated that President Lincoln was not initially a proponent of the emancipation leading up to his Presidential ascendency. Be that as it may, the result of his action fictitiously purged the Red Sea of despair long enough and allowed the captives to go free.

The future they faced was dark, bleak and uncertain. They were left to sojourn in a land without money, land, education, or the social skills essential to adapt to their uncertain embrace. The majority of them were left to wander as pillagers in a land that their forefathers had been forced to labor in and upon, and to build an economy of. Notwithstanding the fact there were no laws that could protect against the loss life, limb and the pursuit of prosperity and justice, as they migrated to points of refuge . . . north, south, east, and west, in hopes of securing a footing in the seminal place they called the "Promised Land."

Going forward, we Americans of African descent, despite some of the most harshest of conditions, continued to endeavor and assimilate in various aspects of society, while awaiting the acceptable moment to become acceptable. Immersed in the deep south, many of us thought it to be more prudent and advantageous to try to acquire economic independence upon the land that our forefathers had languished and labored in and upon since the inception of this country that surnamed America, while many of us took flight and migrated north in hopes of securing a better life in the Northern Industrial base. Still others went west with aspirations of finding inclusiveness.

In either event, wherever we sojourned, the reality was that there was fierce opposition to the acceptable moment to be acceptable. In the Deep South, as many of us opted to become share-croppers, and labored upon the land as peasants with the hope that the land would one day become ours. But, lacking in education and the inability to read, we found ourselves at the end of harvest season either breaking even, or deeper in the morass than before with few exceptions. For those who had sought refuge in the promised land of the north, all too often the reality was the same without a proper education and the necessary economic and social skills needed to adapt in an unfamiliar environment. Those who had migrated west found no solace of acceptance in the evolving territories with the threat of both life and limb with each and every advance.

From a political aspect, it was a foregone conclusion that Americans of African descent would seek inclusiveness in the Republican Party since President Abraham Lincoln had signed the document of Emancipation Proclamation in the esoteric way of setting them free. But with the fight for legislation for "Forty Acres and a Mule," and the first Civil Rights Bills of 1875 that included access to public education and public accommodation, the fierceness of the White backlash dominated the outcome. Still many Americans of African descent remained steadfast in the belief that from a political standpoint the Republican Party was the vehicle that would prosper us economically, educationally, and socially.

But no amount of perseverance or fortitude could erase the stigma of a Negro (blackness). Regardless of how high we sought to attain, spiritually, politically, educationally, or socially, the impediments remained the same. No matter where we sought refuge, there were those who would be in opposition to our advances. There were no laws to protect us from murder (lynching), rape, theft, illegal incarceration, etc. No protection against life and limb.

Prior to, during, and after the civil war, Americans of African descent espoused to demonstrate their allegiance to this country with bravery and heroics, as exemplified with the actions of Crispus Attucks, the Massachusetts Infantry, the Buffalo Soldiers, and the Tuskegee Airmen; still the bravery and heroics remained an acute obstacle of inclusiveness.

Prior to emancipation in the spirit and resoluteness of the Moses' of Denmark Vesey, Fredrick Douglass, Nat Turner and Harriet Tubman, whose aspirations were that the human beings of Americans of African descent would once again be elevated from the dead, after having been cut off from the essentials of language, customs, traditions and spiritual connections, to reemerge and find prominence among the human family. Their plights were to dispel the myths that we were intellectually, psychologically, emotionally, physically, and spiritually inferior by those who knew better, but who had to find justification for their deceit by altering the pages of history in a monstrous attempt to perpetuate the fiction of White Supremacy.

In the aftermath of the emancipation, there emerged numerous Joshua's such as, Sojourner Truth, Josiah Walls, Joseph Rainey, Robert Smalls, Mary McLeod Bethune, Prince Hall, George Washington Carver, Booker T. Washington, Marcus Garvey, Langston Hughes, Louis Armstrong, Jack Johnson, Jessie Owens, A. Philip Randolph, Adam Clayton Powell, James Meredith, Meager Evers, Elijah Muhammad, Rosa Parks, Thurgood Marshall, Rev. Martin Luther King, Jr., Stokely Carmichael (Kwame Ture), Fannie Lou Hamer, Joe Louis, Jim Brown, Malcolm X, Mahalia Jackson, James Baldwin, Leontyne Price, Sidney Poitier, Rev. Jesse Jackson, Rev. (Ambassador) Andrew Young, Minister Louis Farrakhan, General Colin Powell, President Barack Obama, and countless others who in their own right have tried to free Americans of African descent from the debilitating shackles of psychological, emotional, and spiritual impediments of slavery.

Be it in education, politics, sports, economics, entertainment or social consciousness, each of these Joshua's have in measurable ways tried to uplift and inspire us as we have wandered in the wilderness in pursuit of the Promised Land.

Over the past one and a half centuries, Americans of African descent have pursued and assailed to highest heights in education, spirituality, politics, business, sports, and entertainment, and every other endeavor in-between. With each and every attainment or accomplishment, we have been stigmatized with accolades and platitudes of the First Black this and the First Black that as though we are trophies to be presented for others ingratiation or satisfaction while still awaiting for the acceptable moment to be acceptable.

With each step or measure, Americans of African descent have wandered spiritually, educationally, psychologically, emotionally, politically and economically to assimilate into various aspects of society to substantiate our existence and to discard or dispel the spiritual, emotional and psychological shackles of bondage. Some Americans of African descent, in futile attempts to climb the social and economic ladder of the hierarchy of needs and wants pursued a life of crime in which has always led to a dead-end street. But if the truth were to be told, there has been nothing mystical about Americans of African descent having assailed to the highest heights in any endeavor or capacity because it has always been there innately through our genesis from the beginning of time.

Having been denied access to Forty Acres and a Mule, we as Americans of African descent have sought inclusiveness in the creation of the public education, public accommodations, the new deal, integration, civil rights and voting rights, the great society, all of which have allowed us to find improvements in our spiritual, social, educational, and economic status, in which have led to various classifications and measures, such as quotas and affirmative action in order to bridge the gap in economic and educational disparity.

Prior to integration, we Americans of African descent, out of necessity experienced many examples of Black Wall Street, some more prominent than others, but within each of our communities, we had the cohesiveness to establish schools, churches, businesses, and social outlets that survived through our own patronage. Even though integration has had positive effects and advantages from educational and social aspects, financially it has a decimating effect on our communities.

During the civil rights movement the mantra of Self-Empowerment and Unity were prominent elements in our attempt to solidify and substantiate our validity in a society that our ancestors had labored in bondage to initiate and establish in the economy of America. Hence, it appears that we have lost our way again. The mere mention of the word "Unity" terrifies some who continue to appease those who feel offended that you would have the intellect or capacity to do for *yourself*. And have had the audacity to opt and adapt the attitude of go for self or it's about me . . . notwithstanding that they stand on a pyramid of shoulders to have climbed to the height that they have soared.

Never mind the fact or the mention of our African ancestral connection. Some of us have dismissed or bristled at it out of ignorance.

It is no longer important while others who have had no affiliation with it, have the audacity to claim it as their own.

Immediately after the civil rights movement and the great society, many programs were initiated to combat poverty, unemployment, illiteracy, etc. as a result, there were revenues allocated to be generated within our communities to alleviate those disparities afflicting our communities, but at the end of the day, most of those allocations never remained in our communities because we disbanded our communal structure to chase the White Flight, in which have left us vulnerable in view of the present financial debate that faces this nation. Daily we hear about statistics relevant to our community and the results are alarming. All of the gains that we thought we had made seemed to be diminished. Now, we have the highest in unemployment, median income and home foreclosures that have eaten away at the wealth that we thought that we had achieved.

After the passage of the civil rights laws, there emerged many in our local communities, particularly in the South who were placed in positions of power and authority and classified as "Black Leaders," who prior to the struggle of black liberation had been informers and saboteurs of the civil rights moment or struggle; appeasers of the White Supremacist mindset who were no more than wolves dressed in sheep's clothing simply to weaken or illuminate the possibility of strength through unity. Be it politics or economics, these types of individuals or personalities are exemplified or epitomized in the personalities of Supreme Court Justice Clarence Thomas, and former Presidential candidate, Herman Cain, and all of those Black Republicans who lend credence to the devices or schizophrenia of the aspirations of the Tea Party.

On his dying bed, Kwame Ture admonished the Americans of African descent's leadership of the importance of economic and political unity in advancing the well-being of African American's, in which is exemplified in Americans of the Arab and Indian descent who have come here and cornered the markets in the hotel industry, oil and gas facilities within our communities who in fact, will never find trying to establish residence within the African American communities.

Lately, in his efforts to bring about economic parity for all of the citizens of this country, President Barack Obama have suggested the establishment of community banks or institutions that will have a more immediate input in local communities. Maybe it is time the African American communities take a more aggressive and progressive posture in restoring the economic fabric for the next generation(s) of African Americans. As exemplified in the example of the late Mr. A.G. Gaston of Birmingham, Alabama who owned a Savings and Loan Institution in the early fifties and the countless others who tried in various fashions to foster the importance of collective empowerment.

It has been said that in unity there is nothing that these people can't accomplish that they set their minds to do! Over the last half century African Americans have accomplished in all aspects of society that what we have set our minds to do, but what is lacking is the willingness to remove the shackles from the mindset of the Willie Lynch Theory as divide and conquer. Maybe now it is possible to find and anecdote to insulate us from the debilitating phenomenon and finally in these perilous times of economic paralysis and uncertainty, African Americans can set into motion a plan of action that will enable us to establish economic prosperity for the next generation(s) to aspire to.

Lastly, it has become apparent that there are efforts underway to either curtail or eliminate all of the efforts that have been made in the area of politics, to stipend or diminish our voices with the establishment of arcane rules, to discourage, suppress, or alienate our voting potential across the nation, in particular, in the bowls of the Southern Strategy of the South. It is amazing to watch on Saturdays and Sundays how much our children are cheered as they are running up and down the fields and floors of many arenas that fill the coffer with their exploits, yet, there are efforts presently underway to silence our voices in the political arena, those of your grandparents, mothers, fathers, sisters, brothers, nieces, nephews, and cousins.

During the last three years I have listened intently and with emotion and dismay to the many venues of the extreme right who pride themselves in having illuminated many of the Democratic Representatives from office; to include the Blue Dog democrats of the who by the way, have been thorns in the side of President Obama's efforts and also the Moderate Republicans. Daily we hear the rancor of concerns among and within the African American communities about all of the efforts that are being devised to make it difficult or impossible for us to do what we helped to accomplish in the Presidential election of 2008. But then, you allowed President Obama's 'hands to be tied and to be sent to the gallows' of political paralysis and chaos, when you didn't return to the polls in 2010. And for all the chatter that I hear about or within the African American communities, your choices are of that of farts in the whirlwinds, unless you make your voice heard by participation on November 6, 2012. Know this, any American of African American descent that lends any support to the aspirations of the Tea Party is nothing or less than your enemy.

In the end, African Americans from the spiritual, political, economic, educational, social, and emotional aspects of our communities, as members of the human family, must sit around the table of brotherhood, intellectually with compassion, wisdom, and in a spirit of *love*, in the time that is now and for the future, and answer the concept of the age old question, "What would Jesus do?" Then move forward with 150,000 and multiply 25 x 50 million, behind you there will be a multitude. [1]

---

[1] Psalms 82 "God standeth in the congregation of the mighty; he judgeth among the gods. How long will ye judge unjustly, and accept the person of the wicked? Selah—Defend the poor and fatherless: do justice to the afflicted and needy. Deliver the poor and needy: rid them out of the hand of the wicked. They know not, neither will they understand; they walk on in deafness: all the foundations of the earth are out of course. I have said, ye are gods and all of you are children of the most High But ye shall die like men, and fall like one of the princes. Arise, O God, judge the earth: for thou shalt inherit all nations.

Conclusion

Where Have You Been?

The impetus or inspiration for the writing of this book was an outgrowth of sensational resonance of hollow innuendos, vitriol, caricature, propaganda, disrespect, delusions, bellicose and licentious lamentations that emanated with the sound and fury of the onslaught that was filled with bitterness, hatred, envy and jealousy from the hot pot of steam that merged from the heated and divisive rhetoric of the acidic and tangled Tea Party.

Who could have known that when President elect Barack Hussein Obama, and First Lady, Michelle, were embraced and enthralled in the enthusiasm of the fun and pageantry of the festive atmospherics emanating from the coronation of numerous occasions, especially the mobility in which he and Michelle danced graciously before the world? There was the electric crowd that cheered with euphony upon President Obama's oath of office. But, imagine clandestine in the dark hearts, minds and souls of some Americans who in their despair vehemently opposed the Presidency of the first American of African descent, to the point of unfounded nullification.

The clamorous and clownish display of the Tea Party was an extension of the decision that was apparently hatched at the home of George Will. Whereby, President Obama had to be maligned as an ineffectual President at all cost. Later, the message was delivered by the repulsive and demonic mouth of the golden boy in the dark space behind the golden microphone; Rush Limbaugh a couple of days later.

It was out of one of his daily diatribes that were empty and void of substantive value, commensurate of his daily broadcasts that he filtered a dose of hypocrisy and ignorance that keeps his audience perpetually stupefied in the aspirations of the past. Because of his shallowness as a human being, he allowed his ego and pride to utter the effectual words that he "hoped the President will fail." The contrivance of the diabolical scheme was further enunciated by Senator Mitch McConnell, who admonished with impunity that his number one job was to see to it that President Obama becomes a one term President.

It was a calculated, deliberate and devious attempt to choral certain elements of society who were stuck in the delirium of the nostalgic past, predicated on White dominance; even to the detriment of their financial prosperity. Eventually the entire apparatus of the Republican Party contingency felt that it was their obligation and duty to disparage and malign President Obama into oblivion. It was a futile attempt to extinguish the light of *hope* of the torch that had been lit for those who had languished in the mythical darkness, because of the ill-gotten gains of slavery and oppression. Americans of African descent had been falsely stigmatized and marginalized with negative annotations such as sub-human, unintelligent and identified as those incapable of learning with an inability to achieve. But, 'hats off' to all those Americans of conscience and goodwill, regardless of color or creed, who had the fortitude to embrace and accept this positive change for a better America.

The President had spoken eloquently and positively, and with deep conviction of his beliefs and hopes of a united America, to which he extended his hand in many respects to try and bridge the gap in American society. But, in some respects, he received a slap in the face. Remember Congressman Joe Wilson of South Carolina and his demonstrative display in the esteemed House of Congress, where he denounced President Obama.

The Presidency of Barack Obama began amidst the most devastating economic collapse since the Great Depression. He faced the dilemma of the excruciating decision to save the backsides of the greedy tyrants of Wall Street with taxpayers investments. A decision that was initiated under the auspices of President Bush's administration, that was synonymously called T.A.R.P., a decision that he made that was opposed by many American citizens, irrespective of their political affiliation.

But the cries of many in the financial sphere were proclaiming that the financial foundation of America was at a catastrophic moment of peril. That disaster had to be averted. Therefore, a rational and prudent decision had to be made. It was a catch 22 moment of the roll of the dice, "damned if you do, and damned if you don't."

President Obama was also challenged with the unfortunate circumstances of tremendous job loss depreciations. A hemorrhaging of job losses that started in the Bush administration of up to 400,000 a month or more. In addition, there was an implosive and looming deficit because of the ill-gotten, erroneous and erratic adventures of two unpaid wards that the majority of the American people had sanctioned. An unpaid drug prescription plan, a dying automotive industry and an unfair tax advantage for the wealthy and rich that were all based on factual computations, but the problems Americans were facing did not begin in the immediacy of the moment.

It was a direct result of decades of neglect by our political leadership across the board, Democrats and Republicans, who had closed a *blind eye* to the corporate colonization of some of our financial entities, had taken the bet and had decided to plan and initiate the off-shoring of jobs to China and points elsewhere after President Richard M. Nixon created dialogue with China to mine the untapped resources of its cheap labor-force via low wages that would enhance their portfolios of profits, and the disenfranchisement of the American worker of the liberty of the pursuit of happiness.

Then, there was the myth of the trickery of trickledown economics that was prescribed by President Ronald Reagan, to pull oneself up by the bootstraps when one had no shoes. It was part of diabolical attempt to decimate the rights of workers to collectively bargain, an investment that had been the catalyst in the establishment of the middle class. It was a time when the Yuppies had gravitated to the aspiration of upward mobility to this philosophy, which consequently gave them the S & L Crisis, later Enron, and lately, the financial fall of the house of cards known as Wall Street. In any event, the same ingredients of greed, malfeasance and stupidity that led to demise was lacking in wisdom.

What wisdom went into the sanctioning of legislation that enabled financial entities and individuals to expatriate well needed capital for the upkeep of roads, bridges, education, energy concerns, social security, health care, etc. to be stored in off-shore accounts while having the audacity to espouse the virtue of patriotism? Not to mention the perks of insider trading.

Prior to his Presidency, President Obama tried desperately to allay some of the fears of the pressing problems facing this nation. Never mind the fact he had saved the 'hides' of the scoundrels of Wall Street. He also fought for an economic stimulus package to revitalize our fragile economy and he received it. But to the consternation of some detractors who believed that was not enough and for others, that it should never have been done. Remember the fight for legislation for the Health Care Bill, the Dodd/Frank and the Community Protection Agency that received vigorous opposition from aspects of our political leadership and some of their ardent, misguided and misinformed followers (who if they would admit it now with truth and honesty based on factual and empirical evidence), demonstrates that these measures have served them in a positive way.

With the election of 2010, we witnessed a dramatic and tragic change in the political landscape but, before then, there was the election of Senator Scott Brown in Massachusetts, where the people of that state decided to nullify the achievements of the late Senator Edward "Teddy" Kennedy in his pursuits of nationalized health care. Thus, President Obama and this country were denied a pivotal vote in pursuing vital legislation to keep this nation moving forward. At the same time, the Tea Party membership was having a tantrum about the excesses of government and their avowed inclination to take their country back. *Back to what?* Back to a time when human flesh was used as the catalyst for the establishment of the economic system of America, known as capitalism. At the same time some of the framers of the constitution were well known slave holders. Back to a time when brother fought against brother during the Civil War to further its despicable enforcement of slavery, or the genocidal annihilation of the Native American in pursuit of "Manifest Destiny." Back to a time, immediately after the Civil War when the Klu Klux Klans applied terrorist tactics to keep Americans of African descent, perpetually ignorant, politically and financially disenfranchised. Or back to a time when the majority of the American populist was uneducated, to the days when poverty loomed large during the great depression and to the time of segregation and Jim Crow. Back to a time when the United States Supreme Court usurped the will of the people, and selected George W. Bush as President of the United States of America. Back to a time when a President misled the Americans to participate in an illegal war, and the foolish notion that the surge was the primary reason that the war was finally coming to an end, when in fact it was because of those missiles crashing the Green Zone during the summer of 2007, and the determination of the Iraqi people not to become an occupied nation. Recently, when a Prime Minister of another country could have the audacity to ridicule, disrespect, and demean President Obama on national and international television and for Prime Minister Benjamin Natanyahu to be hailed and assailed by idiots such as Rush Limbaugh and Sean Hannity and other Right Wing Conservatives as a hero, as though he was the President of America. All in all, it was a concocted effort to delay the inevitable shift of White domination.

Leading up to the election of 2010 we had the moment of the Independent voters under the leadership of John Avlon and others, who believed that divided government works best. The aftermath led to contentiousness in government that was never witnessed before with the insurgency of the malicious Tea Party. A divisive entity that was willing to bring the country to the brink of financial default, or its continuance to advocate for tax breaks for the rich, Corporate welfare, the disenfranchisement of the middle class and the use of antiquated, archaic, devious and diabolical measures to deny American citizen their right to vote.

On November 4, 2010, I arrived at the polling station at Johnson High School in Huntsville, Alabama at approximately 6:15 a.m. 45 minutes before the polls were to open. The longer I sat the more disenchanted I became with the sporadic influx of citizens awaiting their opportunity to vote. I sadly reflected on two years earlier when I arrived at the same location, and had ventured to the end of the line that extended to the road and was wrapped several times leading up to the building. After I had voted, I returned to my car and listened to radio station WHRP 94.1, as Tom Joyner of the Tom Joyner Morning Show was pleading with his listeners to get out and vote. He was followed up by Toni Terrell, a local host on that same station, and later in the day there was Michael Baisden of the Michael Baisden Show. They all espoused the virtue to replicate what had happened two years hence, but when the tally came in the following morning and the statistics were apportioned demographically, it was unfortunately determined that a large percentage of Americans of African descent sat on their behinds and had not gone out to vote.

Later, it was discovered that those citizens that Chris Matthew of Hall Ball (MSNBC) referred to who live in what he considers as the Rust Belt (Ohio, Wisconsin, Pennsylvania, Indiana, and Michigan), soon learned that they had been hoodwinked in the hysteria of the Tea Party Movement mystique. It became evident that they had been manipulated and exploited to think that the Republican Party was their friends. Ooosp, they were hit with the revelation that the Tea Party explosion that led to the election of fanatical figures into local, state and national government, had already put into place schemes to deny them of their legal rights to collectively bargain, and for some in particular, those in Michigan, within the African American communities, the nullification of their elected officials also include measures that would deny Americans their right to vote.

The result has led to a shrinking Middle Class, poverty on a large scale, median income diminished, high unemployment, low wages and the richer getting richer at the expense of the 99%.

All of which when examined of its unintended consequences, can be summed up in the verse of the recent song, that is sung by the soulful songstress, Chrisette Michele, as it relates to President BarackHussein Obama, "Blame It On Me, Say It's My Fault!"

Blame it on me that because of your vote apathy that I inherited an intransigent House of Congress that has paralyzed me with political paralysis. Blame it on me that you continue to vote politically and financially against your interest. Blame it on me that the low value voter, and uneducated voter of the Rust Belt and the South (White) who by the way should be the most educated people in the world, after having enjoyed four centuries of privilege who have decided that I will not receive their vote in 2012 even though I have tried in many respects to bring the country back from the abyss of financial ruin, that was not of my making back into order. Blame it on me that American Republicans of African American descent are oblivious to the nostalgic virtues and aspiration of inclusiveness of the Party of Lincoln in the present time, has lost its flavor. Blame it on me that the teachers of this Nation, who are the provenance of all learning in the cultivation of minds that has led to any endeavor of success, ironically are underpaid. Blame it on me that the Hispanic immigrants have toiled here for the last four decades for Capitalist exploitation are now being asked to deport themselves.

Blamed it on me that former President George W. Bush and most of his inner circle that led us into a misguided and illegal war, and because of it they cannot travel outside of this country, out of fear of being arrested and charged with war crimes against humanity. And now, Republican Party Presidential candidate, Mitt Romney has put some of those same Neo-Con Zealots on his foreign affairs team to once again hoodwink the American people into another war. Blame it on me that because of the dubious and irresponsible decision of the United States Supreme Court of the Citizens United case that our political process is bought and paid for by the highest bidder. Go ahead, blame it on me that incubated in dubious and vexatious minds of Karl Rove and Frank Lutz are born the instruments of deceit that have been given life that has been allowed to flourish over the last three decades that is reminiscent of the Willie Lynch Theory. Blame it on me that you didn't have your Arab spring in 2000 when the Supreme Court usurped the will of the people and selected a President of these United States and in the words of Republican Presidential Candidate Newt Gingrich who suggested they should be arrested. Blame it on me that many African American religious leaders that hurried to favor President Bush in 2004, and misled many Americans of African descent to vote for a man who had the blood of the innocent on his hands, simply because of their affinity to the Faith Based Initiative Program. Blame it on me that those votes in Indiana, Wisconsin, Ohio, and Michigan has been awakened from their slumber to realize that they were duped by the contrivance of the Tea Party in 2010 who continue to protect the Aristocrats of this Nation, wink, wink, the Koch brothers and such. Blame it on me that three fourths of the players that comprise the football teams across this nation who with their athletic prowess help to secure national championships. Most are from the communities of Americans of African descent that motivates and inspires their patrons to fill the stadiums on any given Saturday, contributing to the enrichment of the coffers of the endowments of these universities. But in a twist of irony some of these patrons advocate, endorse and defend re-enacted measures to disenfranchise and suppress Americans of African descents great-grandparents, grandparents, parents, siblings, nephews, nieces, and cousins of the right to vote.

It is obviously a recurrent of the Jim Crow laws of the strategy of southern politics to render the Democratic Party and Americans of African descent proper representation. As evidenced by the election of 2010, when many of the Blue Dog Democrats were purged from office, of which some others that remained became turn coats and allied themselves with the Republican Party, an act reminiscent of some of the occurrences of the eighties and nineties. It was an exploit that has been bragged about by a local radio host, Dale Jackson of the Dale Jackson Show (WHRP 92.5) in Huntsville, Alabama who hails and assails himself as a kingmaker of politics after he had helped to defeat the turncoat, former Congressman Parker Griffith in 2010. Go ahead yall, just say it's my fault!

Now we look to the next several months of political debate to determine who will lead this country forward. In anticipation we, can peer over the horizon of the political landscape that will be indicative of strife, innuendos, propaganda, vitriol, misinformation, exploitation, racism, and manipulation that will put the citizens of this nation's families against families, father against mother, brother against sister, nephew against niece, color against color, and state against state. We need to save the soul of this country. It is a decision that will have lasting implications on the consequences of our actions or inactions. Will it be an outcome for the protectionist voices of the rich and wealthy, the tyrannical and greedy voice of Wall Street, or the expatiators of wealth to offshore banks in order to avoid their civic duty of paying their fair share of taxes? To include the voices of some of our political leadership, who lend credence to the notion of continued dominance of the American Aristocracy or will it be the huddled voices of those crying out in the wilderness in Ohio, Michigan, Wisconsin and Indiana, who feel aggrieved by the betrayal of those in the Republican Party who have attempted to take away their right to collectively bargain for wages and other benefits that gives hope in the pursuit of happiness. Will it be the discontented voices of the occupiers, the impoverished, the 99%, the children of White America who cast their lot with President Obama in the past election and because of it they are also being denied their right to vote. Maybe it will be the voices of those in the Hispanic community that harvest the food that we consume daily who are now being asked to self-deport themselves or the Americans of African descent who have witnessed President Barack Obama being maligned, disrespected, dehumanized simply because of the color of his skin, which goes to the core of some of the opposition he faces, Racism! The outcome of which, only your vote will effect on November 6, 2012. As Gladys Knight iterated about the soulful sound of the group, Boyz-2-Men, she exclaimed, "They finally got the message!" Maybe then, we will be able to usher in our autumn of deliverance. Where we will proclaim as Rev. Al Sharpton of "Politics Nation" (MSNBC) often does, "Gotcha."

Appendage

LIST OF AFRICAN AMERICAN INVENTIONS

AIR CONDITIONING UINIT: FREDERICK M. JONES; JULY12, 1949

AIR SHIP: J. F. PCKERING 1892

ALMANAC: BENJANIN BANNEKER 1791

AUTO CAR COUPLING FOR TRAINS: ANDREW BEARD 1897

AUTO CUT-OFF SWITCH: GRANVILLE T. WOODS; JANUARY 1, 1839

AUTO FISHING DEVICE: G. COOK; MAY 30, 1899

AUTO GEAR SWITH: RICHARD SPIKES; FEBRUARY 28, 1932

BABY BUGY: W. H. RICHARDSON; JUNE 18, 1899

BICYCLE FRAME: L.R. JOHNSON; OCTOBER10, 1899

BISCUIT CUTTER: A. P. ASHBOURNE; NOVEMBER 30, 1875

BLOOD PLASMA BAG: DR. CHARLES DREW; 1945

CAPS FOR BOTTLES AND JARS: A. E. LONG & A. A. JONES; 1898

CASKET LOWERING DEVICE; A.C.RICHARDSON; NOVEMBER 3, 1894

CELLULAR PHONE: HENRY I. SAMPSON; JULY 6, 1971

CHAMBER COMMODE: T. ELKINS; JANUARY 3, 1897

CLOTHES DRYER: G. T. SAPSON; JUNE 6, 1862

COMBINED FURROR OPENER AND STALK KNOCKER: G. W. MURRY

CURTAIN ROD: S. R. SCATTON: NOVEMBER 30, 1889

CURTAIN ROD SUPPORT: WILLIAM S. GRANT AUGUST 4, 1896

DOOR KNOB: O. DORSEY; DECEMBER 10, 1878

DOOR STOP: O. DORSEY; DECEMBER 10, 1878

DUST PAN: LAWRENCE P. RAY AUGUST 3, 1897

EGG BEATER: P. JOHNSON; FEBRUARY 5, 1884

ELECTRIC LAMPBULB: LEWIS LATIMER; MARCH 21, 1884

ELECTRIC RAILWAY TROLLEY: ELBERT R. ROBINSON; 1880'S

ELEVATOR: ALEXADER MILES: OCTOBER 11, 1867

EYE PROTECTOR: P. JOHNSON; P. JOHNSON NOVEMBER 2, 1820

FIRE ESCAPE LADDER: J. W. WINTERS; MAY 7, 1878

FIRE EXTINGUIHER: T. MARSHALL; OCTOBER 26, 1872

FOLDING BED: L.C BAILEY: JULY 18, 1889

FOLDING CHAIR: BRODY & SURGWAR; JUNE 11, 1889

FOUNTAIN PEN: W. B. PURVIS; JANUARY 7, 1890

FURNITURE CASTER: O. A. FISHER; 1878

GALOSHES: A.L. RICKMAN; 1898

GAS MASK: GARRETT; OCTOBER 13, 1914

GOLF TEE: T. GRANT; DECEMBER 12, 1899

GUITAR: ROBERT F. FLEMMING, JR.; MARCH 3, 1886

HAIR BRUSH: LYDIA O. NEWMAN; NOVEMBER 15, 1800's

HAND STAMP: WALTER B. PURVIS; FEBRUARY 27, 1883

HEATING FURNANCE; ALICE PARKER; 1918

HORSE SHOE: J. RICKS; MARCH 30, 1885

ICE CRÈME: AUGUSTUS JACKSON; 1832

ICE CRÈME SCOOPER: A L. CRALLE; FEBRUARY 2, 1883

IMPROVED SUGAR MAKING: NORBET RILLIEEUX; DECEMBER
    10, 1846

INSECT DESTROYER GUN: A. C. RICHARD; FEBRUARY 28, 1899

IRONING BOARD: SARAH BOONE; DECEMBER 30, 1887

KEY CHAIN: F. J. LOUDIN; JANUARY 9, 1894

LANTERN: MICHAEL C. HARVEY; AUGUST 19, 1884

LAWN MOWER: L. A. BURR; MAY 19, 1889

LAWN SPRINKLER: J. W. SMITH; MAY 4, 1897

LEMON SQUEEZER: J. THOMAS WHITE; DECEMBER 8, 1893

LOCK: W. A. MARTIN; July 23, 1800's

LUBRICATING CUP: ELLIJAH McCOY; NOVEMBER 15, 1895

LUNCH PAIL: JAMES ROBINSON; 1887

MAIL BOX: PAUL L. DOWNING; OCTOBER 27, 1891

MOP: THOMAS W. STEWART; JUNE 11, 1893

MOTOR: FREDERICK M. JONES; JUNE 27, 1939

PEANUT BUTTER: GEORGE WASHINGTON CARVER; JUNE 27,
    1896

PENCIL SHARPENER: J. L. LOVE; NOVEMBER 23, 1897

PHONE TRANSMITTER: GRANVILLE T. WOODS; DECEMBER
    17, 1884

RECORD PLAYER ARM: JOSEPH H. DICKERSON; JANUARY 8, 1819

REFRIGERATOR: J. STANDER; JUNE 14, 1891

RIDING SADDLE: W.D. DAVIS; OCTOBER 6, 1895

ROLLING PIN: JOHN W. REED; 1864

SHAMPOO HEADREST: C.O. BAILIFF; OCTOBER 11, 1898

SPARK PLUG: EDMON DBERGER; FEBRUARY 2, 1839

STETOSCOPE: IMHOTEP; ANCIENT EGYPT

STOVE: T. A. CARRINGTON; JULY 25, 1876

STRAIHTENING COMB: MADAM C. J. WALKER; 1905

STREET SWEEPER: CHARLES B. BROOKS; MARCH 17, 1890

THERMOSTAT CONTROL: FREDERICK M. JONES; FEBRUARY 23, 1960

TRAFFIC LIGHT: GARRETT MORGAN; NOVEMBER 20, 1923

TRICYCLE: M.A. CHERRY; MAY 6, 1886

TYPE WRITER: BURRIDGE & MARSHMAN; APRIL 7, 1885

Bibliography

Barnes, Jack. After Slavery: The Fight for Forty Areas and a Mule. The Militant. New York

Browder, Anthony T. Nile Valley Contribution to Civilization. The Institute of Karmic Guidance. Washington, D.C. 1992.

Davis, Tan. To the Edge of the Universe. Towery Publishing, Inc. Memphis, TN. 1999.

Fox News, Timeline. September 11, 2001. Thursday, September 12, 2003.

Gate, Eras. Public Education in the South. Encyclopedia. 2010.

Grim, Ryan. Public Option Amendment Failin Senate Finance Committee. Huffingtonpost.com. December 12, 2010.

Grimmett, Richard, Ackerman, David. International and Domestic Legal Issues Relating to Use of Force.

Hartmann, Thom. How an Earlier Patriot Act, Law Brought Down a President. commondreams.org. June, 2003.

Hamby, Alonzo L. The Imperial Years: The U.S Since 1939. Weybright and Talley. New York. 1976.

Jeff, Boomer. The Obama Stimulus, Month 15 Progress Report. Google. May 2, 2010.

Mason, Lindu. CBS Coverage of Election Night 2000. The Anneberg School for Communication, University of Pennsylvania, January 2001.

Marcono, Tony. Private Gains but Economy Sheds 125,000 Jobs. NPR. July 2, 2010.

NGO Forum at Durban Conference 2001. NGO Monitor Report. November 25, 2009.

Oak Ridge, Tennessee, Wikipedia. The Free Encyclopedia. 2010.

Peebles, James W. Ph.D. The Original Heritage Study Bible, King James Version. The James C. Winston Publishing Company. Nashville, TN. 1993.

U.S. Refuses to Deal with Its Legacy. Province Journal (RI). August 31, 2001.

Walsh, Susan. One Call Too Many, News. New York. November 14, 2000.

WE MUST CONTINUE TO FIGHT

We were brought here
In balls and chains
Beaten and oppressed
We were put through the test
The test of torture
To be made ignorant;
Ignorant of our native land;
Ignorant of our native tongue;
Ignorant of our heritage;
But we bore the burden,
We beat the ship,
We did it with our mothers, fathers
grandmothers, grandfathers,
great-grandmothers, great-grandfathers,
Blood, sweat, and tears
We made it through the most painful years.
We did it with hope, faith, and determination.
We were determined to be free
To enjoy this world that God has made for all.
We have fought the battle of yesterday,
and we won.

But the war goes on
We must continue to fight,
As long as we have life,
We must continue to fight,
But let it be with honor, dignity, and pride.
Let words be your weapon,
Let words be your enemies' defeat;
Let words fight as long as words can.
But when words will no longer do,
Do what you have to do,
Be brave, bold and strong.

Franklin V. McQueen

Xenoph Company
Presents

Franklin V. McQueen earned his B.A. Degree in Journalism from Benedict College Columbia, South Carolina in 1979. He is the author of two books;" Horizons, The Beginning and the End" and "Once Forbidden". Both published by Author House Bloomington, Indiana. He is currently completing his third book "Dilemma, America in Motion," which is schedule for public in September 2012. He is also a poet who has recited his poetry on stage, television and radio. To include his poetry being published in several news papers.

Franklin is a native of Bennettsville, South Carolina where he received his early education in the Marlboro County public school system.

His books can be purchased @Authorhouse.com, Amazon.com, Barnes & Nobles.com and BooksA.Million.com website.

For immediate purchases, his books are sold in the Café's gift shop inside the Embassy Suite Hotel & Spar, 800 Monroe Street Huntsville, AL 35801. Home phone number: (256)715-1425 Cell number: (256) 653-7961. Email: McQueenF23@yahoo.com.

+ Ideals + Belief + Faith + Initiative + Work + Determination = Capital

www.ingramcontent.com/pod-product-compliance
Lightning Source LLC
Chambersburg PA
CBHW020244290526
45784CB00003B/1096